What to Do If You Find a Cougar in Your Living Room

Self-Care in an Uncaring World

By

Rose Bak

WHAT TO DO IF YOU FIND A COUGAR IN YOUR LIVING ROOM

© 2020 by Rose Bak

About This Book

If you found a cougar lounging in your living room, would you run? Or would you hang out with it peacefully? The way you answer this question may be the difference between being generally happy or generally miserable.

How do you find happiness in your current life? It's a choice, and it starts with you. You taking care of yourself. You doing the work. You trying something and if what you try doesn't work, trying something else. Forget trite self-help advice about bubble baths and smiling, this is self-care for the real world.

"What to Do If You Find a Cougar in Your Living Room" is a collection of bite-sized essays on stress relief, feeling good in your body, managing anxiety, active self-care, mindfulness, setting boundaries and living your best life.

Each chapter includes journal prompts to help you think about how to make the information work best for you. Grab your copy today and learn more about how to care for yourself in an uncaring world.

Be sure to join Rose's mailing list. Click here[1] to be the first to hear about all the latest releases and sales.

---

1. **https://bit.ly/rosebaknews**

Dedication

For Missy, because sometimes the best self-care is having a kindred spirit.

Introduction

Are you sick of self-help "gurus" telling you to take a bubble bath to relieve stress or to smile in the face of adversity? Me too. I live in the real world where there's stress.

A few years ago I was generally miserable. Pessimistic. Stressed out. Overwhelmed. Then I turned fifty and decided that I didn't want to live that way anymore and so I launched my "I'm 50 Now Self-Realization Tour". My goal? To stop wasting time being an Eeyore.

I changed jobs. I became a certified yoga teacher. I started meditating. And best of all, I started writing. I wrote about real ways I was improving my attitude. I wrote about how sometimes the best thing for your mental health is to divorce your family. I wrote about how breathing or stretching made me feel better. I wrote about how I was sick of hiding my imperfect body. I wrote about....life. Life as a middle-aged woman on a quest to be happy.

"What to Do If You Find a Cougar in Your Room" is a collection of some of my most popular essays. Each chapter also includes some journal questions to help you consider how to incorporate the advice into your own life.

I hope you enjoy these essays and that you too can live your best life feeling happier, healthier and more content.

What to Do If You Find a Cougar in Your Living Room

Hint: Don't run. Just like a lot of things in your life, it's not as scary as you think.

Despite what you might be thinking, this is not about an older woman dating a younger man.

I read a news story about a woman in southern Oregon who discovered a cougar relaxing in her living room. That's right, an actual cougar wandered in, hung out and took a long nap.

At first I thought it was a hoax because these days I have a hard time telling the difference between the Onion and actual news. But it was covered by several local media, and I was able to find the woman's Facebook posts with the story to confirm.

The short version is, this woman left her front door open to keep her house cool, and unbeknownst to her, a cougar was in the neighborhood and decided to stop by for a visit.

Now, like me, you might hear that and be thinking, wow, that poor woman probably wet herself and called animal control in terror, and then they came with a sedative gun and knocked out that cougar.

But no, that's not what happened.

The woman, who describes herself as having extensive experience working with animals and doing energy work, wasn't scared at all. Instead of calling animal control, she used vibrational energy to telepathically communicate to the cougar that it was safe in her house. She says she looked at the animal with a loving gaze, making eye contact, as she communicated with it.

Apparently reassured, instead of eating the woman, the cougar settled in behind the couch and took a six-hour nap while the woman sat in vigil.

Finally, six hours later and needing to leave, the woman gently woke up the cougar with drumming. She said she raised her vibrational frequency and telepathically sent the cougar a message about how to exit the house by visualizing his path to get to safety. Then the cougar got up and happily ambled out.

The woman described the whole thing as a "blessed encounter".

Now if you don't live on the west coast, this story probably sounds insane to you. But as someone living in a very New Age state, it actually doesn't sound that hard to believe. Just another day in Oregon.

I couldn't figure out at first if this woman is a cougar whispering hero or totally foolish. I've decided it's the former, and I kind of want to be her new best friend.

Think about it for a minute: something happens that by most people's definition would be totally terrifying. But she rolls with it and is totally calm and nonjudgmental. Instead of responding with fear and doing something that would injure the animal, she responds with love and has a very profound spiritual experience.

How many times do we approach a situation with fear because we're conditioned to think it's scary? You might see a dog on the street, or a teenager who looks shifty, or a cougar in your living room, and immediately make an assumption that they will hurt you.

You respond with fear, and you send that fearful energy out to the universe.

Maybe they pick up the energy you're sending and act as you expect them to act. Or maybe they don't, and you wasted that energy for nothing.

Maybe you missed out on an interesting opportunity to learn something about another living being.

Of course, there are lots of dangerous people and situations. I get that, I grew up in one of the most dangerous cities in the country. Just yesterday someone showed me a photo of a murder that his sister witnessed in another country. The world can be dangerous, it's foolish to think otherwise.

If we approach everything as if it will be dangerous, if we make a snap judgement about what's dangerous, we miss out on a lot of potentially great experiences.

If the woman in this story had approached the cougar as dangerous, she would have missed out on learning more about the beautiful creature.

I challenge you, as I challenge myself, to start with love, not fear.

Give people the opportunity to rise to your expectations, not fall to your judgment.

You might not ever get the opportunity to communicate with a cougar in your living room, but there are plenty of other profound experiences waiting for you if you just open yourself up to them.

Reflection Questions:

- *Think of something you used to be afraid of but are now comfortable with. What did you learn from the switch?*
- *What things would you experience if you put aside your fears?*

My New Career as a Yoga Model

Why I'm Done Hating Pictures of Myself

I have always hated pictures of myself. Maybe it's because I'm shy and introverted. Maybe it's because of a lifelong dissatisfaction with my size and my looks. Maybe it's because I'm a vampire....just kidding, I'm not a vampire, everyone knows vampires don't show up in photos. Anyway, I'm always the person ducking down at events when a photographer comes by, hiding in the back at a group photo, sidling away when someone wants to take a picture.

When I am in a picture, my lifelong pattern has been to critique myself. First of all, like the titular character in My Name is Earl, my eyes are always shut, unless I do a wide eye crazy face but even then, somehow the photographer usually catches me in a blink.

Secondly, I am then compelled to ruthlessly judge my looks in the picture. And I mean compelled. I catalog everything I hate: how large I look, how flat my hair is, how my clothes hang on me, how large I look in comparison to others, how much more attractive the others are, why I'm not smiling, if I am smiling how I hate the way my teeth look, why my eyes are closed, how old I'm looking....it goes on and on. Seriously, sometimes it's exhausting to be in my head.

But I had a little epiphany a few weeks ago as part of my "I'm 50 Now Self-Realization Tour". I was doing some cleaning and decluttering and found my old high school and college year books. I haven't seen them in probably 20 years, so I eagerly looked through them to see memories of my long-ago youth. And I looked. And I looked.

I discovered that there are very few pictures of me in my yearbooks. I guess I wasn't surprised, but I was disappointed. Some years I apparently skipped class pictures so there's no little headshots of me with my classmates. And even though I was involved in so many activities in both high school and college—honor society, newspaper editor, yearbook staff, Latin club, French club, multiple clubs—I'm mostly absent from the pictures. There was very little "me" in my history. I wound up recycling those yearbooks.

The sad thing is I know I'd look back at Young Rose and think she was a cutie, but there's very little evidence to support this. Even though the advent of Facebook and Instagram has meant that I'm now capturing photographic evidence of my life, I realized I was still caught in the avoiding/criticizing picture loop.

I was so appalled I decided then and there I was going to stop being so freaked out about pictures, stop cataloging my faults, and start embracing my photos. If people don't like the way I look in a tank top, they don't have to look. If my eyes are closed, so what, I thought. I'm resolved to be brave and look for things I like in my photos, the way I would if I were looking at a photo of a loved one or a friend.

Wondering if I was all talk? Yeah, well, within days of my epiphany, an opportunity came along to test my resolve. My yoga studio was looking for students to pose for new photos they could use for social media and other purposes. They were specifically looking for a variety of ages, sizes, races, and disabilities. I thought, I love yoga. I don't look like a "typical" yoga person. And I fully credit yoga for keeping me from being fully handicapped (I have bars immobilizing about half my spine, leading to lots of pain and lack of movement). Without giving it too much thought, I immediately e-mailed the studio owner and said that I was interested.

I then proceeded to dither about it for a few weeks until the photo shoot. Would I have the guts to go through with it? I actively tried to counter every fear with a "so what?" What if I look too fat in these pictures? So what, fat people can do yoga. What if I look too old? So what, yoga is great for reversing the effects of aging. What if there are unflattering shots of cellulite or fat rolls? So what, most people have them, and if people don't like it, they don't have to look.

Photo shoot day came. We were supposed to wear a plain white shirt, so I purposely went with a tank top to challenge myself and my self-judgement of my arms. I fixed up my hair carefully, spending more than my customary five minutes in order to get it looking great. My friend did my make-up, something I rarely wear. And before the shoot I did a little self-love kindness meditation in the car to get myself in the right frame of mind and calm my nerves.

And you know what? It was fun. I didn't feel too awkward, especially after we got going. I often feel awkward in new situations, so that was good. I tried to relax and not think about what I looked like or where things were sagging or rolling. I tried to just be. Be present. Be me.

A few weeks went by and I'd almost forgotten about the photo session. Then I went to sign up for class yesterday and I saw it: they had updated the website and there was a picture of me. I did a double take, the way you do when you see something you're not expecting. And then I thought, wow, what a great picture! I look cute! I look strong! I look flexible! That was seriously my first reaction. As I studied it, instead of categorizing what looked "bad" about me in the picture, I consciously itemized all the cute factors: my smile, my little pink feet, the great form of my pose, my flexibility, the shiny fullness of my hair.

I look great. I actually like a picture of me. It's empowering. It's revolutionary. And I totally want to be a yoga model now.

Reflection Questions:

- *Look at pictures of yourself. Are you hiding or out and proud? Really study your image in the pictures. Name at least three positive things about the picture.*

- *What would you do if your body met your vision of perfection? Would you dress differently? Act differently? Be front and center in all your pictures?*

Put Your Hands in the Air and Show Yourself You Care

How the simple act of lifting your body up towards the sky can help you feel better.

One day early on in my yoga teaching career I was leading my fellow yogis through a series of sun salutations.

There were some beginners in the class, so I broke down the flow of poses into segments and spent some extra time on each section. The series started with a position called "upward salute", which is essentially standing up straight with both feet on the floor and lifting your arms overhead.

I cued the pose and looked around the room — almost everyone was lifting with scrunched shoulders and a small movement just involving their arms. I catch myself doing this all the time as well, but I didn't realize until I was facing the class how common that was.

I offered the cue to lower the shoulders and stretch up using the whole body, lightening the weight of the feet. As the students opened up their spine into a full body stretch, I saw people's faces relax. Everyone seemed to grow taller.

The energy in the room seemed to shift. It was amazing.

It made me curious. How did one change make such a huge difference?

There are many great benefits to this seemingly simple pose. Even if you've never stepped foot on a yoga mat, you can get some significant benefits from an upward salute. It's a pose you can do with no training and no special equipment.

Do this anywhere.

- Get up from your chair and stand with your feet about hip distance apart.
- Center your weight over your feet. Stand up straight with your head aligned over your spine, and the crown of your head lifted.
- Stretch your hands above your head without scrunching your shoulders. Lift up with your whole body, energetically moving every part of your body upward.
- Stand still in the position for at least 30 seconds and breathe deeply.

For me, this motion feels like when I was a kid and I'd hang from the playground equipment at the park, a lovely all-over body stretch. Some of the benefits of this action include:

- Creating space in your spine, easing compression, and counteracting some types of back pain
- Increasing energy
- Loosening tight shoulders
- Opening your chest
- Improving your posture
- Counteracting the forward lean of the neck we get from staring down at devices all day
- Strengthening muscles throughout your body
- Improving balance
- Improve circulation
- Helping food to move through the intestines
- Reduce stress and anxiety
- Making you feel strong and empowered

Sometimes you can do one simple thing that makes a big difference, and this is one of those things. Even if you take only one minute for yourself today, you will still see a benefit. So put down your computer, get out of your chair, and stretch!

Reflection Questions:

- *How often do you stretch up to the sky? Why keeps you from stretching your body more?*
- *How does it feel to take up space? When do you find yourself making your body small?*

I Have No Complaint Whatsoever

How complaining only leads to more things to complain about.

Today I was reading the story of a woman Zen master named Sono. She was known for her practice of leading people to enlightenment by using the affirmation *"Thank you for everything, I have no complaint whatsoever"*.

People would come to her ill, upset, suffering, and still she told them to use this affirmation and repeat it often. Understandably a lot of people thought she was crazy to say this in the face of people's pain and suffering, but those who followed her advice found healing and contentment. Why?

When you drop all your complaints, you truly begin to appreciate all that you have.

When I read this, I thought of my grandpa. When people would ask him how he was, he would often say, "I've got nothing to complain about, and even if I did, no one would care anyway."

Grandpa's point, like Zen master Soto, was that in the scheme of things, most of us have little or nothing to complain about and sharing your laundry list of complaints is not the least bit interesting to others. My grandpa was a very wise man.

Why share your litany of minor complaints with those who have their own complaints? The fact is, no matter what bad things you experience, there's always someone who has it much worse. You have no idea what others are dealing with.

There's no suffering Olympics, we all have things we have to deal with. There's no prize for having the suckiest life, and if there was, I can guarantee you that you would not win. You wouldn't even place. Neither would I.

My mother was a master of the suffering Olympics. I once observed her complaining about how hard it was that her husband didn't make enough money — to someone whose husband had been out of work for two years and was about to lose their house. Another time she complained about how uncomfortable the hospital chairs were, to someone who was in the recovery room after a painful surgery.

I think we all know someone like this. Their experience is so tragic in their own minds that they cannot entertain the possibility that others are in worse straits. They thrive on being a victim. Their constant want for something more blinds them to the blessings in their lives.

What if instead of choosing to focus on all that's wrong in your life, you choose to focus on all that's right?

What if you were to thank the universe for everything you have, and instead of focusing on what you want, you focus on what you already have?

"Thank you for everything, I have no complaint whatsoever".

People talk a lot about gratitude in November, and that gratitude is almost always about something good that's happened. "I'm grateful for my promotion". "I'm grateful my son was accepted into college". "I'm grateful the offer was accepted on my house". "I'm grateful my dog got hit by a car."

What if you express gratitude for the less pleasant things in your life, the ones that actually made you stronger, taught you something important, made you realize what's important?

"I'm grateful for my divorce because it helped me learn to be independent". "I'm grateful for my heart attack because it gave me a wake-up call to focus on my health". "I'm grateful for my bankruptcy because it taught me how little money I really need".

"Some of god's greatest gifts are unanswered prayers." — Garth Brooks

Try it today. Sit in a quiet place, close your eyes, and spend at least a minute listing everything that you're grateful for. Then spend another minute listing things that helped you grow, even if you weren't happy about them at the time.

If it's easier, use a journal. It doesn't have to be something fancy, just a spiral notebook will work. Set aside five or ten minutes a day to reflect on not just the things you are easily grateful for, but also those things you came to be grateful for over time.

It's a powerful way to refine your gratitude practice.

Find a way to feel gratitude for everything in your life, good or bad, and you'll find peace.

"Thank you for everything, I have no complaint whatsoever".

Reflection Questions:

- *Name ten things you are grateful for right now, no matter how small.*
- *Think of something that was bad at the time but turned out to be a blessing in disguise. What did you learn from the good that came with the bad?*

How to Tap into Your Creative Side

Even if you don't think you have a creative bone in your body.

I'm going to tell you a secret: for most of the first 50 years of my life I labored under the misconception that I wasn't creative.

I don't know why I thought this about myself, but it was likely a combination of a few things.

First, I was never good at, or even remotely interested in, arts and crafts. Grammar school art class was only marginally less horrible than the gym. It seemed like a waste of time when I could be learning "real" things.

I never looked at a piece of paper and felt compelled to draw.

I couldn't read music and I wasn't drawn to any instruments.

I never felt compelled to paint a picture or do Papier-mâché or knit or sew a quilt.

I would look at my grandma and my godmother, who were super crafty, and feel perplexed at how they thought of things and how they had the patience to work on things. Seriously, they would take a wine bottle and turn it into a Little House on the Prairie door stopper. They would take styrofoam and beads and make the most beautiful Christmas ornaments. They were incredibly creative.

As an adult, I know a lot of creative people.

My roommates are both super creative, and they bond over things like visits to the fabric store, and I've never understood it. Two of my friends are married to accomplished full-time artists who make a living with their art. I know a couple of authors, some illustrators, a great singer, and a guy who plays the ukulele on his breaks at work. I have looked at them all enviously, thinking, "I wish I was creative".

I thought there was some creativity gene I was missing.

When I was younger I used to love to write poetry and short stories. I wrote quite a lot and I loved it, although I didn't think of it as being creative.

Then there was an incident in high school where the nun teaching my English composition class decided my creative writing was "too dark". Instead of encouraging me to explore my creativity, she sent me to chat with the school nurse about whether I had suicidal thoughts. Then she called my parents to talk about what was "wrong" with me that I was writing about grim topics.

My writing was clearly "wrong", so I stopped doing any creative writing. My creative flame was extinguished.

Instead, I got into journalism, which was one of my majors in college. I edited the high school and college newspapers, and also worked at a local newspaper.

Journalism, despite what certain politicians might argue, is the opposite of creative writing. I was taught to write the facts, and only the facts, with no creative embellishment. As I moved through my career I've done a lot of grant writing and technical writing, which is again very fact-based.

I went along for years feeling sad that I was not creative.

But then a couple of years ago I turned fifty and started what I called my "I'm 50 now Self-Realization Tour". I started thinking a lot about what gives me energy, what nurtures me, what I've always wanted to do and haven't.

That's when I realized I missed writing.

I missed the creativity of looking at a blank page (or screen) and making it come alive with stories or information. And so, I began writing for the first time in over 30 years. I created a blog. I wrote some romantic fiction. I started publishing on Medium and other sites. I made a commitment to write at least 30 minutes every day.

Suddenly, it was like I shook up a can of Coke and popped the top: ideas were bubbling out everywhere. I have a running list of things I want to write about.

Now I'm always working on multiple writing projects. I'm writing fiction, poetry, essays, non-fiction — I'm writing anything that appeals to me.

I also started honing my craft. I joined writers' groups and attended a couple of writers' conferences because — I'm a writer now. I'm super excited about my last three years of actively writing. It's been the perfect balance to the responsibilities and stress of my demanding grown-up job.

I now understand that it's not that I wasn't creative, it's that I was defining creativity too narrowly and refusing to recognize what my brain wanted to do.

I ruthlessly pushed down my creative urges and focused on what seemed like more mature pursuits. But after three good years of writing, I firmly believe that we are all creative — we just need to find the best outlet for our creativity.

There are so many positive benefits of creativity.

Engaging in creative pursuits helps keep your brain young and healthy by creating new neural pathways. It's a great stress reducer. It encourages innovation. It increases self-confidence. It helps with problem-solving. It's satisfying. It's fun.

If you are convinced, like I was, that you're not creative, I encourage you to prove yourself wrong. Here are some ideas to spark your creativity:

- Take some classes that appeal to you, like painting or macrame or drumming, and see what that sparks.
- Think back to when you were a kid, like I did, and remember what creative things gave you joy when you were young, then try those. Was it coloring? Play-doh? Light Bright? Who cares, just try it.
- Do some meditation focused on engaging your creative brain.
- Listen to music.
- Dance.
- Try one of those adult coloring books.
- Buy a xylophone.
- Become a patron of the arts.
- Perform at an open mic.
- Something will resonate with you if you look.
- Sit down and finally start on that great novel that's been kicking around in your head forever.

When you find something that appeals to your creative side, go for it. Go big. Don't judge yourself or compare yourself to others.

You might be the worst painter ever, but who cares, as long as it makes you happy? Your knitting might look more like a rag than a scarf, but that's OK you accomplished something. You might sing off-tune but go ahead and belt out that song like you're practicing for your Broadway show.

It's all about finding joy and tapping into the creative side of your brain. Don't let the judgmental nun in your head keep you from your joy.

Embrace your creativity. Find your passion.

___

Reflection Questions:

- *What art or craft activity did you like as a child? What if you did that right now?*
- *How does your fear of not being "good" at something prevent you from being creative?*

The Secret to Maintaining Your Equilibrium in the Bad Times

How to get through it when life throws you a curveball.

Last year my dog got hit by a car. It should never have happened — he was on a leash, walking in the crosswalk, and had the right of way. A person turned and clipped him in the crosswalk, claiming to not have seen the giant white dog or the full-grown man walking him. Fortunately, she did not hit the dog walker, but Edison, my dog, was hurt.

Instead of the fun walk, he was expecting, Edison wound up spending the day in the hospital in great pain, leaving with a bunch of stitches, road rash, a couple of prescriptions, and the "cone of shame".

When he came home Edison limped around the house in a drug-fueled haze, appearing very confused and upset, knocking things over like a white Godzilla.

He had lost his equilibrium.

It was a reminder of how you go along living your life and all of a sudden something unexpected happens, knocking you off-balance, possibly changing your life forever.

There's a pandemic. Someone you love dies. You get laid off. You lose your lease. You have a serious health scare. Your partner leaves you. You get hit by a car.

Suddenly, in a moment, everything changes.

When faced with unexpected bad news, how do you react?

Some of us are a bit fatalistic, and we say things like "Well, I knew that something was bound to happen eventually."

Some of us try to find meaning and reason to make sense of what happened. "Everything happens for a reason, I just need to figure out what I am supposed to learn from this."

Some of us feel like a victim and get angry, asking "Why does everything bad happen to me?"

After something knocks you down, it's important to focus on restoring your personal equilibrium. The bad things that happen in life help you build resilience if you let them.

Here are some things to think about building your resilience and moving forward:

- *Self-Care:* You've had a trauma, be kind to yourself. Don't beat yourself up. Try to eat well and get rest. Take time to feel your emotions. Avoid things that are numbing but make you feel worse in the end, like excessive drinking or eating.

- *Learn the Lesson:* Many people believe that there's a lesson in everything that happens. Ask yourself, what is the universe (or God, or whatever you believe) trying to tell me? For example, a health scare or death of a loved one might be a wake-up call for you to take better care of yourself, or a car repair may remind you to engage in more preventative maintenance.

- *Build Connection:* Whatever you're going through, someone else has had that experience too. Talking to people about your situation might help you find others who had that same experience, and they may be able to offer valuable suggestions for moving forward. For example, talking to others who've gone through a divorce can help you prepare for what's coming and how to cope. And even if people have no clue what you're going through, a kind, empathetic listener can make all the difference.

- ***Let Go of Anger:*** We all need some time to vent from time to time but holding onto anger isn't healthy. The stress is bad for you physically, and it impedes your ability to see clearly and move forward. Regardless of whether the thing that happened was preventable, it is what it is. I can be angry at the woman who hit my dog, but that doesn't change my almost $800 vet bill, and it doesn't help him recover any faster.
- ***Focus on possibilities and choice:*** Assess what choices you have and focus on what you can do to move forward. It might not have been your choice to have a heart attack, but it can be your choice to have another. You might be devastated to have lost your job but look at the possibilities of new career options.

Is any of this easy? Of course not. But you can continue to rail against the situation like Edison does with his cone of shame, or you can settle in and figure out a solution, like pulling on that cone until the velcro rips open and you're free.

The choice is yours.

Reflection Questions:

- *Think of a time when something threw you off balance and you lost your equilibrium. What things kept you grounded? What do you wish you had done at the time to help yourself get through it?*
- *Where does your mind go when something unexpected happens? What fears and emotions does it bring up?*

Why Won't You Stop Crashing into the Window?

Why stubborn persistence isn't always the way to go when you encounter a challenge.

One day when we were all still working face-to-face, I stepped into a coworker's office to ask her something. There was a loud and distinct thump. We both turned towards the noise just in time to see a bird fly right into the window.

We watched in growing horror as the bird would crash into the window, fly backwards, hover for a minute, then rush forward and crash into it again. And again. And again.

"How many times is he going to do that?" my coworker wondered. At least twenty, as it turned out. No exaggeration.

"Wow, he's really got some persistence," I said. "But how do we get him to try something else before he hurts himself?"

We decided to pound on the window and see if startling him would snap him out of his obsession. It worked, and the little guy flew off to find a different path.

While I initially admired the little bird's persistence, later I realized he was making the same mistake many of us make: he committed to a path and kept on with it despite all evidence showing it was the wrong way to go.

Instead of learning from his mistakes, he kept making the same exact mistake over and over again.

How many times do we stay in a job, or in a relationship, or pursue a goal with stubborn determination long after it's clear to everyone around us that it's the wrong way to go? How many times do we ignore that voice in our heads that tells us that we need to do something different?

Sometimes it's about ego. We're embarrassed that we are on the wrong path or in the wrong relationship and everyone realized it before us.

Let's face it: we all hate to be wrong. It's hard to have to go back to the people who told you years ago that your boyfriend was a jerk and admit they were right, but it took us longer to get there.

Or we tell ourselves, well I have already invested so much time into this goal/idea/relationship, it has to pay off eventually otherwise all this effort was wasted.

You've likely heard that Thomas Edison failed 1,000 when inventing the lightbulb but he also kept trying a new design. Imagine if he was like, "I'm just going to keep on re-doing this same prototype because I've already invested so much in it, maybe it will work this time."

Sometimes we feel like we are expected to remain committed to someone or something, and people will judge us if we don't. This can happen especially when you have to make the hard decision to cut yourself off from members of your family.

Sometimes it may be because while we're in this "definition of insanity" loop, at least it's comfortable.

We know the good and the bad, and trying something new....a new job, a new apartment, a new relationship, can seem overwhelming.

And maybe sometimes we just have some dogged optimism that we're right. Look at how many people get into pointless argument on social media, because they're sure they convince someone that they're wrong.

It's a good thing to persevere and keep trying. People have achieved great things when no one thought they could, and all signs indicated that they would fail. We all love those underdog stories about how someone walked into tryouts and landed an NFL gig or was rejected by fifty publishers before someone took a chance and published their soon-to-be-a-bestseller book.

And then again, there was that episode of Friends where Monica's boyfriend decided he could be a UFC fighting champion, despite his lack of athleticism, and was continually beat up without ever improving.

"Stay committed to your decisions but stay flexible in your approach." — Tony Robbins

---

The question is, how do you know if you're on the right path or not?

Take a lesson from the little bird: regroup between failures, consider your approach, and if someone is pounding on the window giving you a warning, at least listen to the warning and give it some consideration.

You may choose to continue flying into the window, but at least do it knowing that you have all the information.

Reflection Questions:

- *Think of a time when being persistent led to a success, and another time when your persistence turned to stubbornness. How were the two situations different? How did you finally decided to try something different?*
- *What questions can you ask yourself to avoid falling into a stubbornness trap?*

Am I Too Old for This?

Why you should stop asking for permission and start living life on your own terms.

The older I get, the more I hear other women my age judge things in relation to their age. "Am I too old for this?" they ponder. "Oh, no, I'm too old to do that," they say.

"Am I too old to wear this outfit?"

"Am I too old to wear my hair this long?"

"I'd love to take that class/go on that trip/learn that new thing, but I'm too old."

It's an interesting paradox because I also frequently hear women over fifty talk about how things have changed for them now. They have discovered a freedom that comes with age.

"I used to suck it up when I experienced sexism, but now that I'm older, I speak up."

"I used to never leave home without makeup, but now that I'm older I don't care."

"I used to never wear tank tops, but now I don't care if people see my arms."

So which is it?

Does being over fifty give us freedom to do what we want? Or does it bring new self-imposed restrictions?

I think the answer is a little bit of both.

For many of us, we've stopped caring so much about societal expectations and being liked. Women over fifty are much more likely to be activists, to overtly embrace feminism, to find their voice and speak up when things aren't right.

Yet some of us still struggle with not wanting to look like some pathetic middle-aged woman who can't act her age. We don't want to wear the tight miniskirt or low-cut blouse that we embraced in our youth.

It seems a little desperate, like we can't accept our age. We don't want to be that sitcom stereotype.

If you google "dress your age" you'll find hundreds of articles encouraging you to embrace your older, more conservative wardrobe. I call bullshit on this. You know what, if you want to wear a miniskirt or a halter top or heels, you do it. If you like it and feel comfortable, you do it anyway. Don't give a thought to what people think.

I'm convinced that this "dress your age" stuff is really about continuing to control women's bodies.

Sure, you might be a fat or saggy or wrinkly, so what? In a culture that embraces thinness and youth, wearing something that doesn't hide your "flaws" is an act of rebellion. If people don't like your dimpled thighs, they can just not look.

Use your newfound lack of giving a damn about people's opinions to help you live your life on your own terms.

If you don't care if people see you at the Trader Joe's without make-up, don't care if they see you there in a tweety bird baby tee and cute wedges.

If you are sick of sexism, be sick of people telling you how to dress.

If you don't care if people see your grey hair, don't care if they realize you dye it orange.

If you're sick of being Ms. Nice Woman when people are rude to you, stop being Ms. I Care What People Think in all areas of your life.

I'm here to tell you, it's not too late to do what you want to do. You have raised your kids. You're probably established in your career. You know what you like and what you don't.

Be happy, be comfortable, embrace your freedom.

You have one life. This is YOUR time now, live life to the fullest and live it for YOU, not anyone else. Dedicate this second part of your life to doing whatever you always wanted to do. Do the things, wear the things, enjoy the things that will give you pleasure.

Take that class. Travel. Go to that trendy club and dance like no one's watching. Wear your hair long, wear pigtails, paint purple stripes in your hair. Date that younger man or woman. Go back to school.

Live with no regrets my friend. Be that totally cool crazy old woman who people secretly envy. That's what I plan to do.

Reflection Questions:

- *What's the difference between how you dress now and how you dressed when you were younger? Why did this change?*
- *When you think about dressing differently than you do now, maybe something shorter or tighter or more colorful, what feelings does this bring up for you?*

My Robot Vacuum is Surprisingly Wise

41

Important Life Lessons from the Machine that Sucks Dirt Off My Floor.

One of my best middle-of-the-night purchases was a robot vacuum.

I had been contemplating purchasing one for a while, so it wasn't exactly spur-of-the-moment, but looking at the dog hair on the carpet late one night convinced me that it was worth a try.

If you haven't seen them, the robot vacuum is a handy little self-propelled machine the size of large pizza that cleans your floors.

It's no muss, not fuss — all you have to do is program it and periodically empty the tray. The robot vacuum is fully programmable — it starts, stops, and recharges automatically. If it gets stuck or the tray is full it will give you helpful warning beeps but otherwise it just does its thing.

Because I have an innate need to anthropomorphize things, I named the robot vacuum Reggie. Reggie the Robot. I know, I'm super creative.

At first, she acted like I was crazy, but I have even got my roommate calling it Reggie now. "Where's Reggie?" she will ask if she doesn't see him wandering around cleaning. The other night she came out of the bathroom and I heard her say, "Oh hi Reggie."

Reggie may be a machine, but he exemplifies some important life lessons for all of us.

Never Give Up.

Reggie can be determined. A little stubborn even. When he runs into a corner or gets trapped under the couch, he keeps turning and moving until he finds a way out to freedom. If he runs into an obstacle going in one direction, he adapts and tries another.

He doesn't upset, he just keeps persevering.

It's a good reminder that we often run into obstacles, but sometimes we just need a different perspective. Looking at a problem another way can make all the difference in finding a solution.

Psychologists point out that how you perceive obstacles can impact your ability to address them. Like Reggie, keeping your emotions out of it can help you address challenges more logically and effectively.

Dialectical Behavior Therapy offers a method called STOP that can be helpful when you hit a roadblock. STOP stands for "Stop, Take a step back, Observe, and Proceed mindfully".

This technique can be a good way to take your emotions out of the picture and think about the problem in a more neutral way as if someone else was facing it.

You don't have to give up, just change your perspective and try something different. We've all had the experience of being "stuck" on something. When we distract ourselves or take a different approach it can make all the difference.

Keep to a Consistent Schedule.

Reggie wakes up every night at 6:55 p.m. — mostly because I couldn't get the remote to land at a 7:00 p.m. wake-up, but that's totally user error. He moves through the same rooms of the house, keeping the same speed, until 8:25 p.m. when he starts heading for his charger.

His workday is short but effective. When he works, he works. When he's not working, he's not working. He doesn't work overtime or vary from his schedule.

Humans, like robot vacuums, like consistency and routine. Keeping a balance of scheduled time for work, rest, and leisure is the key to good mental and physical health.

A consistent schedule is even more important now when many of us are working from home. The lines between work and home are more blurred than ever.

Sticking with a daily routine can reduce your stress levels and improve your mental and physical health. An important part of maintaining a routine is reducing decision fatigue.

The Journal of Personality and Social Psychology published a study that found that every time you make a decision, you add stress. Creating a regular flow of your day and routinizing things like meals and daily habits will be beneficial.

You don't have to schedule every second of every day but setting boundaries on your day can really make a difference — for you and for your family. Don't forget to schedule some "me" time.

Take Time to Recharge.

The robot vacuum is programmed to head back to his charger as soon as his batteries are drained. He returns to the dock and with a little beep, Reggie rests as he recharges his battery.

How often do we continue to work and press on even after our human batteries are drained? Taking time to rest is important for us all.

Mental Health America identifies sleep, relaxation, and exercise as the three main keys for keeping yourself healthy and dealing effectively with stress.

Experts recommend that adults get 7–8 hours of sleep each night, and quality of sleep is almost as important as quantity. It's a good time to overhaul your sleep hygiene, recommit to a bedtime schedule, and give your bed a little update to make it more comfortable.

While there's no set recommendation for how much you should relax, you should definitely find some time to relax every single day. Whether it's yoga, meditation, listening to music, enjoying hobbies, or even taking a hot bath, relaxation helps release stress, decrease pain, and improve mood.

Another stress reliever? Exercise. You have heard this before: experts recommend that you get some exercise most days. A mixture of aerobic exercise, like cardio, and strength training will provide the best benefits.

Ask for Help When You Need It.

When Reggie needs help he doesn't hesitate to ask for it. He's not ashamed to seek outside assistance.

After he's exhausted his known solutions, Reggie sends out a signal to let me know he's in trouble. When I hear his beeps I know that he is stuck somewhere, something is trapped in his rollers, or his collection bin is full.

Asking for help can be difficult for most of us. In many cultures, we are raised to be rugged individualists who are self-reliant. But sometimes we can all use a little help, whether it's from a friend, family member, mentor, or outside expert.

There are benefits to seeking assistance when needed, including developing new skills, creating empathy, and increasing connection with others. Asking for help also can benefit the person who's assisting — we all like to be needed and feel useful.

M. Nora Bouchard, an executive leadership coach and the author of "Mayday! Asking for Help in Times of Need" says that people often hesitate to ask for help because they don't want to give up control, appear needy, or be rejected.

She suggests keeping framing your need as a conversation about a difficulty instead of an outright request — often people will step forward to help without you asking.

Other tips including keeping your requests manageable, building a support team, and making sure that you reciprocate when someone else is in need.

There's no shame in needing help sometimes — we all do. Just be sure to ask for help before your problem gets to a crisis point.

Cleanliness Reduces Stress

Reggie is a surprisingly effective appliance for day-to-day cleaning.

I have a dog who sheds more than you would ever think one animal could shed, and I used to vacuum all the time. Now, I let Reggie handle the day-to-day work and I do a "big vacuum" with the upright every five to seven days.

Clutter and mess can be damaging psychologically. It increases our sense of overwhelm. Conversely, addressing your clutter can make you feel better.

In a survey of 2,000 adults conducted by OfferUp, they found that 61% of Americans report feeling less stress after tidying up and 54% of people report feeling relaxed after cleaning.

You don't have to have floors you can eat off of, but a few minutes of daily tidying can make a big difference. Make your bed. Put dirty dishes right into the dishwasher. Wipe up the sink. Pick up your dirty clothes. It can all make a difference in how you feel about your environment — and your life.

My recommendation? Get yourself a robot vacuum. Reggie has made a big difference in my life, and he will help you too.

Reflection Questions:

- *Think of an area of your life where there is literal or virtual clutter. How does it make you feel? Imagine how it would be different if that clutter were magically gone.*
- *Are you comfortable asking for help when you need it? What holds you back?*

Why Adult Friendships Matter

How you can maintain relationships and meet new friends as an adult

When I was in grammar school we learned a song, it went: "Make new friends, and keep the old. One is silver and the other's gold."

This song, which appears to now be in the public domain, was intended to teach kids that friendships are precious and meant to be mutual.

The older I get, the more I appreciate the friendships in my life.

When you're young, it's pretty easy to make friends, especially when you're still in school and there's a wide variety of people in your age group. I remember in high school and college I had a wide circle of friends from various groups, and a couple of "best friends".

We were all so close, and in our youthful optimism sure we would be "best friends forever". Then we all graduated.

Some people moved away, some got married and started families, some focused on their careers, and for the most part, those friendships faded away. Until we all joined Facebook years later, I had no idea what became of most of the people I hung out with when I was younger.

It can be sad to think of those long-lost friendships and the absence of people from your life who were once so important to you.

Adult friendships are tricky. It's more difficult to create new friendships and find new potential friends.

As adults, most friendships seem to come from work, parents of your kid's friends, neighbors, or couples you hang out with. You don't have endless hours to hang out and get to know people like you did when you were a kid.

I think we've all had the experience where you had a really good friend at work, then one of you moves on and that's it for the friendship. Or you were good friends with your husband's best friend's wife, but then one of the couples splits up and the relationship is lost. Or you felt close to someone then they dumped you as a friend as soon as there was an issue between you instead of talking it out.

Those separations hurt for sure, but in the end, you have to wonder if you were really friends at all.

Adult friendships are crucial to our mental health. Having friends can increase your level of optimism, decrease loneliness, get you out of the house even when you're feeling down, and provide crucial support when life gets hard. Friends can be energizing and open you up to new experiences.

Studies have shown that there is increased well-being and happiness among adults who have at least five meaningful relationships.

How do you develop meaningful friendships as an adult? Since you can't just go up to random people and say "will you be my friend?" as you did as a kid, you have to find other ways to add to your circle of friends. Here are some ideas:

- **Join a club:** When I started running, I became involved in several running groups. I made some good friends through those groups, a few of which have survived the test of time. It doesn't have to be just running, other ideas to try: book club, writing group, adult sports league, and knitting groups are just some of the places you can find a new friend.
- **Meet-Ups:** If you watch the "meet up" boards you'll find opportunities to meet people and do anything from hiking to board games to movie nights to wine tasting and more. You have to put yourself out there and meet up with a bunch of

strangers, but they're all there for the same reason as you: to make friends. While many of these are on hold right not due to the pandemic, there are still some socially distanced and virtual events happening.

- **Rekindle Dormant Friends:** Let's say you have a friend you haven't seen in a long time and you miss. Give them a call or send a message and suggest getting together to take a walk, do a catch-up on Zoom or meet for a drink or coffee. It'll be good to catch up and you might realize that they've been missing you too but felt weird about initiating contact after so long.

- **Start Talking to People:** You probably see some people all the time and think they seem nice. Start chatting with that woman who always puts her mat by you in yoga class. Strike up a conversation with that guy who does his laundry at the same time as you. Suggest a happy hour for people at work to get to know each other more. Go to an art event alone and see who else is alone. The worst that can happen is that you have an awkward conversation, but you might also find a friend.

It's also important to put a little effort into maintaining the friendships you already have. I went through a period of time years ago where I was going for a number of friends, but eventually, I realized a lot of those relationships were empty and full of drama.

Now I focus on the quality of my friendships.

The friendships I have now are, for the most part, long-term and absent of any drama or expectations.

I have learned over the years that I don't want drama, and I don't want to have to do all the work to maintain the relationship. If you don't generally feel good hanging out with your friend, it's not worth it. If the friendship is more work for you than them, or frankly if it's a lot of work at all, it's probably not worth it.

Sometimes you just have to be grateful for the good times you had and let go of friendships that aren't working. Like any relationship, being friends with someone shouldn't be exhausting.

In my circle right now, I have some friends I talk to every day, and some I get together with for a drink or a walk every few months. Some I mostly keep in touch with via text.

I have friends who go to yoga with me, friends who go to happy hour with me, and friends who will try out a new class or go to a movie (or did before the pandemic anyway).

I have friends who I know would pick me up if my car was broken down or help me bury a body.

I even have friends who I can go without talking to them for six months or more, then when we see each other we just pick up where we were last time we met, which is awesome.

This happened just last week. I met two friends for a beer on the patio of a brewpub on a warm afternoon. I had not seen and mostly not talked to either of them in at least a year, other than occasional texts. We sat down, caught up, and were chatting as if we had been in contact all along. Simple and easy, enjoying each other's company.

You too are deserving of friends who enrich your life and make you feel good.

Call or text an old friend today. And if you have space available in your life for new friends, put yourself out there a bit and see who's waiting to be your new friend.

Remember, friends are a gift. Appreciate them. And if they don't fit quite right, return them and shop for someone new.

Reflection Questions:

- *Who are your most important friends right now? What positive things do they bring to your life?*
- *Do you have friends outside of your family and workplace? If not, how can you rekindle old friendships or look for new friends?*

Have a Little Faith — in Yourself

Why the fear of things going wrong keeps you from appreciating when things go right.

Not that long ago we had a dharma talk in a yoga class on the subject of faith.

"Like some of you, I had a visceral reaction when I heard that was the topic of the month at the studio," the instructor said. "But then I thought, faith isn't just religion. It's also faith in ourselves."

This led to a discussion of times when it was hard to have faith in ourselves or faith that things would work out well, and our fear created suffering, particularly because it wasn't always justified.

Later in class it struck me that sometimes this lack of faith in ourselves also can interfere with our enjoyment of the present moment.

"Always remember you are braver than you believe, stronger than you seem, and smarter than you think." — Christopher Robin

I don't want to jinx myself, but things are going really well in my life right now. Despite the shitshow that is 2020, I am really pretty content.

And the fact that I felt compelled to start that sentence with "I don't want to jinx myself" is indicative of a problem that many of us have.

When things are going well, I'm often waiting for the other shoe to drop.

You may be thinking, "Hey, that's how life is. Things go well, they go not so well. Life is cyclical and there are always ups and downs".

And yes, you're correct to think that. But for those of us with anxiety, it's sometimes hard to enjoy the "ups" because we're so focused on the "downs" that we know are coming.

This is particularly true in a year that's been filled with more downs than ups.

In the end, it's a question of faith.

Faith that we can handle the downs, the same way we handled the ups.

Faith that if we are struggling in the downtimes, eventually things will look up.

Faith that life isn't just a zero-sum game where every good thing has an equal and opposite bad thing to cancel it out. Instead, there can be more of your life on the "good" side of the ledger.

Being alert to potential bad events is hard-wired into all of us to some extent, but this constant dread that something bad is going to cancel out the good is also a typical byproduct of past trauma.

Past events create the anxiety that bad things are coming because they always do.

So how can we start to break out of this pattern? I was curious about that myself. Here are some suggestions to help you (and me) enjoy the good times and not fear for the future:

- ***Recognize your negative thoughts:*** Sometimes we manifest what we are thinking. If we think something bad is coming, it might, but if we think something good is coming, it might. Re-frame your thoughts to be more positive and less fatalistic.
- ***Acknowledge that your vigilance has kept you safe:*** If your fear and dread of the future is based on past trauma, being on

guard has likely helped you survive past events. Thank yourself for taking care of you.

- *Use mantras:* Repeat words that make you feel strong and safe. Visualize them. Believe them.
- *Take a Breath:* Changes in breath are often the first sign of stress. Focus on keeping your breathing easy. When you have a negative thought, make sure you are breathing. Then breathe out forcefully or r exhale longer than your inhale.
- *Embrace the fact that you deserve good things:* Tell yourself you deserve to have good things happen, and that you deserve to enjoy the good times.

Things are going very well for me right now and that's awesome. I'm healthy, I love my job, I love my friends and I have the freedom to do the things I love, like writing and practicing yoga.

I am going to have faith that everything will continue to go well in my life. I am going to have faith that when life throws me a curveball, I'll still be able to hit it out of the park.

Reflection Questions:

- *Think of a time when someone did not have faith in you, but you knew you were strong enough to succeed. What made you certain that you could succeed?*
- *What things do you trust yourself to do well? What would be needed to convince you to trust yourself in areas where you're less confident?*

You'll Never Write That Novel — or Whatever Your Secret Dream Is

If you can't turn your dream into a passion, you'll never succeed

This weekend I published my 14th book.

After finishing writing the book earlier in the week, I spent part of the weekend editing, formatting, and publishing it on Amazon and then setting up advertising and social media for the new release.

I also updated and published an update on a previous book, wrote five Medium articles that I submitted to publications, taught two group yoga classes on zoom, cleaned the bathroom, walked the dog, and voted.

It was a busy weekend.

"You're so prolific with your writing," several people commented to me. "How do you find the time?"

The answer is simple: I make the time.

Granted, I don't have kids so that makes my time more flexible than many people. But I do have a lot of responsibilities and distractions. I have a full-time and high-stress job. I have high maintenance and active dog. I have an older house. I live with chronic pain. I teach three yoga classes a week.

But I make the time to write because writing is my passion.

For years I talked about how I wanted to be a writer. I had big ideas percolating through my head all the time. But I never made the time. The writing was just a dream.

One day I realized that if I wanted to be a writer, I needed to actually write. I needed to prioritize writing. I realize now that Old Me had a dream. Current Me has a passion, and passion requires sacrifice. Passion requires commitment.

There are some people who live in a dream world, and there are some who face reality; and then there are those who turn one into the other.

Douglas H. Everett

What about you?

Maybe you dream of writing too. Maybe you want to do a triathlon. Maybe you want to learn to play an instrument. Maybe you want to buy a van and wander around the country exploring.

If you want your dream to become a reality, you need to find the passion and energy. The commitment to make it happen.

When I decided to become a writer, I looked for ways to set myself up for success. Here are some tips that I found particularly helpful:

1. **Look at your schedule.** Once you take out the time you are at work and sleeping, how many hours are left? Do you know how you fill that time up? I bet you waste a lot of time watching TV or doom scrolling on Facebook or watching cat videos on YouTube. Track your time for a few days, I bet you'll be surprised how much time you waste. Direct that time towards your passion project and see what happens.

2. **Find an accountability partner.** I used to be a runner and having a partner I met every Saturday for a training run kept me on track. Whatever your passion is, there's a group for that or at least one other person who shares your interest. Search Facebook for groups that are focused on your same

passion. Put out a call to your friends for accountability partners.

3. **Make use of dead space between other activities.** If you have fifteen minutes between other things on your schedule, you have time. Practice a song on the piano three times. Outline an article or write a few paragraphs. Take a ten-minute run. Be efficient.

4. **Use tools and experts.** Ask for help if you need it. If you're not sure how to get started, there is likely a lot of information available for whatever your passion area is. Read a book, watch a YouTube, take training, download an app. There is help somewhere, just find it.

5. **Accept imperfection.** You won't be perfect when you start your passion project. Your grammar might suck. Maybe you don't know a B-flat from a B-sharp. Maybe you are the slowest runner. Who cares? Honestly, you are never going to be the best or most famous (insert your dream title here), but you can be the one who keeps on learning and has fun. And the more you work at it, the better you will be.

6. **Set achievable goals.** You're not going to write a book in one day or go from a total couch potato to triathlete in one week. Figure out what's do-able for you right now, set some mini-goals and start chunking away at your dream. Use lists or online tools like Trello to keep you on track. As you see the progress you will get more excited about your dream — until it's a passion.

What's your passion project? And what are you going to do about it?

Reflection Questions:

- *If anything is possible, what would you do for fun? Are there ways you can fulfil these dreams right now, even with baby steps?*

- *What goals do you have where you have the skills but just never get around to them? How can you convince yourself to go for it? What would you tell a friend who was in the same situation?*

The Key to Contentment

How to find peace and acceptance — even when everything sucks

Everyone around me has been stressed lately — the pandemic, the protests, the election. It's a lot.

I've been reflecting on the subject of contentment. What is contentment? How can I be more content, despite everything going on in the world?

There's a concept in the yogic traditions called "santosha" which I am finding helpful.

Santosha is a Sanskrit world that includes two parts: "sam" which means completely and "tosha" which means contentment or satisfaction. Put together the words convey not only "contentment" but also "acceptance".

Santosha, as I understand it, is not about being mindlessly happy. It's about finding happiness within, despite the circumstances, instead of relying on external factors to make you feel good.

This means instead of wallowing when things go bad, we look for the good in them, and the opportunities for growth.

It's about seeing the silver lining.

We had a discussion in a yoga class about the concept of santosha that I remember well. We talked at length about the role of acceptance in practicing contentment and finding acceptance even when things are not perfect, and how difficult that can be.

For example, I have a disabling back condition and have been in some level of non-stop pain every single day since 1981. I spent a lot of time railing at the world about how unfair it was that I had this condition, why it happened and how I wished it could be different. But over the last ten years or so I've just accepted it.

It sucks, for sure, but I can be content with it, because I've realized wishing to be pain-free isn't going to happen. I make myself more miserable fighting against it. The best I can do is to accept it and do whatever I can do to not aggravate my condition. Coincidentally, yoga is one of those things that helps.

"Be content with what you have; rejoice in the way things are. When you realize there is nothing lacking, the whole world belongs to you. "
— Lao Tzu

Contentment is about accepting people and things as they are, and not dwelling on how you wish things should be. It's about keeping a positive attitude when there are difficulties, and not letting your unfulfilled expectations of a person or situation cause you inner pain.

That's the lesson of the pandemic in a nutshell.

We don't like wearing masks. We miss going to parties and concerts and movies. We grieve when people get sick and we can't comfort them in person. No one likes drive-through graduations or endless zoom calls or virtual happy hours.

But most of us accept that this is the way things are right now and try to find happiness and contentment in the things we can. Things suck right now, but not everything sucks.

We need to focus on the positive things. The simple joy of playing with the pandemic pet we adopted. The delicious bread we're making every week now that we've got time. The new hobbies we started. Time spent outdoors.

Contentment seems to come up a lot in thinking about weight loss and body image. I think many of us have that experience where we look back at a picture of our younger selves and wish we'd been happy about our appearance when we were young and cute and thinner. We weren't content with how we looked at the time where we probably looked the best we ever have.

Now we're firmly in middle age or maybe we've put on some pandemic pounds.

We might find ourselves wishing our bodies weren't sagging, or our stomach was smaller, or that there weren't wrinkles around our eyes. Instead of accepting the inevitability of aging and its effect on our bodies, we continue to create unhappiness by engaging in self-criticism and railing against things we mostly can't change. How would things change if we practiced contentment and accepted that this is our body right now?

We bring a lot of misery and suffering on ourselves wishing things were different.

The idea of santosha isn't that you should just BE content, it's that you should PRACTICE contentment. It doesn't just happen, you have to work for it, you have to seek it.

I find this idea of contentment and acceptance more difficult when it's about accepting other people's behavior.

We all have those things about other people that drive us crazy: the person who's always late, the person who promises to keep a confidence and immediately blabs, the coworker or spouse who doesn't do their share of the work, the person who lets you down again and again.

Here again is an opportunity for growth. As they say, you can't change other people, you can only change how you respond to them. When we expect people to behave differently than they have in the past, we're almost always disappointed.

Our work is to accept them as they are — we don't have to like it, we just have to accept them as flawed beings that we can't change.

We give people emotional power over us and we give them space in our head, but we don't have to do that. It's not so much that the people create the stress for us, it's that we allow ourselves to be stressed by people acting just as we know they are.

By practicing contentment, we can cultivate patience and try to be neutral about their behavior. And if their behavior is truly egregious, or we really can't get to a place where we can accept them as they are, then we need to make a change, not them.

We need to be responsible for our own contentment.

How can you cultivate more contentment in your life today?

Reflection Questions:

- *When do you feel the strongest sense of contentment? Can you bring that same feeling to a different situation? What would it be like to feel content in a less-than-ideal situation?*
- *When something happens that you can't change, what's your reaction?*

Why You Need to Take a Deep Breath Right Now

How focusing on your breath can make you feel better fast

"Breath is the bridge which connects life to consciousness, which unites your body to your thoughts." ~ Thích Nhất Hạnh

This summer the entire west coast is pretty much on fire.

Fire season has been worse every year and those of us who live in this part of the country have spent a lot of time the last few summers talking about air quality and how hard it is to breathe.

Breath is one of those things we don't think too much about until it's a problem.

We go happily along, expecting that when we need to our lungs will expand and bring in the air that we need. Then one day, it doesn't. It's too smoky. We're having an asthma attack or an allergic reaction. We hyperventilate during something stressful. We're choking. We fall and knock the wind out of ourselves.

We panic, because suddenly breath, that thing we don't think about, is all we can think about.

Breathing is super important, obviously. It oxygenates our blood. It removes waste like carbon dioxide out of our system. It helps our cells function. It helps us talk. It produces energy. It helps us live.

Most of us go around not breathing at full lung capacity even on a good day. We tend to breathe with shallow breaths, only using the top of our lungs.

Shallow breathing keeps our bodies from functioning as well as they could and contributes to stress.

Proper breathing uses your diaphragm and completely fills your lungs. It calms your emotions, energizes you, and clears your mind.

So why don't we learn more about breathing?

We know controlling our breath is helpful. How many times have you heard someone say to someone who is really upset, "take a deep breath"? It's because taking a deep breath helps.

I remember years ago I got into the habit of having the occasional stress cigarette. On particularly bad days at work, I'd sneak out behind the building and enjoy what someone I know calls "a smoky treat". I was frustrated with myself about why I was compelled to do this.

I was in therapy at the time and mentioned it to my therapist who said, "Maybe you go out to smoke because the act of smoking causes you to breathe. What if you just went outside and took a moment to breathe without the cigarette?"

I tried going out for a breathing break and it totally worked. I just needed to have a little quiet time to breathe and break up the stress of my day.

In yoga and meditation practices, they teach you to breathe more fully. We learn to take a breath at the top of our lungs, then draw it down until our stomachs expand and we activate our diaphragm.

Often we will place our hand on our lower abdomen so we can feel it move out with our breath. The inhale ends, and the exhale begins, from the lower abdomen.

Sometimes we'll hold the breath in for a few counts before exhaling, other times we'll consciously make the exhale longer than the inhale.

Sometimes we breathe in with our noses and out with our mouths, while other times we only breathe with our noses.

There are different breathing exercises for different purposes, some are more relaxing, some are more energizing, some are cooling, some settle the mind.

Just the act of focusing on our breath helps us to tune into our bodies and relaxes us. Even without conscious effort, our breathing tends to improve just by focusing on it. But add in a specific breathing exercise, use your whole lung capacity, and it can be magical.

Improving your breathing is more important than ever right now. Many of us struggle with wearing masks, struggle with the isolation of COVID restrictions, struggle with the financial and emotional stress of the pandemic. It makes self-care more important than ever.

Try to incorporate some deep, relaxing breaths into your everyday activities. Take a breathing break a couple of times a day — even if you have to set an alarm or appointment to remind you.

If you practice yoga or meditation that's a perfect time, but you can also do it while you're at a stoplight, while you're waiting for a meeting to start, while you're taking a walk when you are feeling stressed or anxious, and while you're trying to fall asleep at night.

The internet is chock full of great resources on breathing including articles, videos, guided exercises, and step-by-step instructions if you need more help.

Now take a deep breath with me and relax.

Reflection Questions:

- *Take a slow deep inhale, filling up your chest. Does it feel weird? Does it bring anxiety? What emotions come up when you slow down and deepen your breath?*
- *What tools can you use to remind yourself to breath more fully?*

How can you prioritize even a few minutes of silent focus each day?

Biting Off More Than You Can Chew: Is It Ambition or Insanity?

How to Decide if Your Goals are Attainable No Matter How Audacious They May Seem

I was walking with my dog Edison the other day and we came upon a little bird. I don't know what it was, one of those little guys with fluttery wings, like a hummingbird or something.

While Edison enjoyed some grass nearby, I watched the bird as it picked up a stick in its beak. The stick was easily three times longer than the bird was. It was huge in proportion to him.

The bird grabbed the stick, started fluttering his wings like mad, rose about a foot off the ground, then sank back down under the weight of the stick. He shifted the stick in his mouth, fluttered his wings as fast as he could, rose about a foot off the ground, then dropped back down. He tried it a third time with the same result.

Then he dropped the stick and took off, presumably to find a more suitable stick.

It reminded me of that old quote that the definition of insanity is doing the same thing over and over again and expecting a different result.

That little bird had a great approach.

He went after a big audacious goal: a desirable stick that was much bigger than him. He tried it to pick it up and failed. He tried something different and that didn't work either.

But after his third attempt failed, he regrouped. He went after a different goal. He presumably didn't beat himself up about, he just moved on.

How many times do we stick with a goal, or a relationship, or plan even when it's clearly not working?

How can we tell when we should persevere, and when we should cut loose?

Here are some things to think about when you feel like you have bitten off more than you can chew, and your goals seem frustratingly out of reach:

Find the "why": Ask yourself why you have adopted this goal. Is it because it's expected of you? Is it because it seems like the next logical step? Is it because that's what everyone else is doing?

I remember talking to someone from my old running group who was training for a marathon and she told me that she hated marathon training. "I don't even want to do a marathon," she wailed.

I was astonished. "Why are you training for one then?" I asked. "Because everyone else in the group has moved from a half marathon to a marathon, it's what you do."

Assess the attainability of your goal: Sometimes a goal is just not in the realm of possibility.

Maybe you want to lose 30 pounds before your vacation next month. That's just not going to happen. Maybe you want to be a singer on Broadway, but you can't hold a tune.

If the goal is simply too far out of your grasp, think about what you can do that's actually attainable. You could potentially lose 5 pounds before your vacation or take singing lessons to learn how to sing Broadway songs in your shower.

Ask yourself, if this goal is just too audacious, what can I do instead?

Consider whether short-term discomfort will pay off in the long term: When you're getting through a bachelor's degree taking one class at a time, or working an extra job to pay off debt, it may seem impossible that you'll ever be done. But you will be.

There is a finish line there, even if it's so far away right now it's just a spec on the horizon. Just keep focused and eventually you'll get there — eventually.

Take a break: If you have been working and focusing on your goals for too long, you may just need a break.

If it's possible, try taking a few days or a week off. Put it totally out of your mind. Rest and restore. Then assess how manageable the tasks are when you go back to them and make your decisions from there.

We all have those times when we feel overwhelmed and the difference between where we are now and where we want to be feels like a million miles.

Follow the example of the bird: try, rest, try again, and if it's not going to work, re-adjust.

Reflection Questions:

- *Think of a time you set an enormous and ambitious goal. Did you succeed? Why or why not?*
- *What are your current goals? Are they attainable? How will you bridge the gap between your dreams and your goals?*

Commit to Non-Random Acts of Kindness

How to Make a Difference in an Unkind World

"Human kindness has never weakened the stamina or softened the fiber of a free people. A nation does not have to be cruel to be tough." — **Franklin D. Roosevelt**

I was walking with my dog Edison and as we passed, one of the neighbors offered us lettuce from their garden. "We have too much," she said, "Please take some. We are probably going to compost it otherwise."

As we walked away with a giant handful of lettuce, I thought about how touched I was by their simple act of kindness.

Kindness seems like a relic of the past, like politeness and good grammar.

The loss of kindness seems related to our lack of connection. We all spend so much time on our devices that it makes interacting with people rarer every day.

Recently a coworker commented about how she was standing in line at the grocery store and when she looked around, every person was looking at their phones. Even those who were with another person or their kids, they were all looking at their phones. "I don't understand why we can't just talk to each other," she said.

As we all turn more into ourselves and our digital lives, it becomes easier and easier to "other" people: the homeless, immigrants, people with different political views. I can't tell you how many people I've had to hide on social media for the last few years due to their hateful posts.

To be clear, it's not about hiding people I don't agree with. I love to hear well-thought-out debates or spend time understanding how someone has come to a different view than mine. I love to agree to disagree with someone who holds differing views than me.

What I don't like is when people are unkind. When they say things that are racist or sexist or homophobic. When they dehumanize. When they talk about other people, people they don't know, like they don't matter. Like they are "less than". Like they are animals or somehow subhuman.

None of us know what it's like to walk in someone else's shoes. No one knows what kind of choice we would make if we were faced with the same situation as some of the people we rush to criticize. It's easy to sit in your nice warm house and judge someone who became homeless, or someone who flees a terrible situation in the country where they live, or someone who gets caught up in a spiral of addictions or abuse.

It's easy to criticize someone who is having the worst day of their life when the biggest annoyance we had today was someone spelled our name wrong on our Starbucks cup or someone cut us off in traffic.

When we get to know other people, it's easier to be kind. When it's someone in your family who becomes an addict, you develop sympathy for how people get in this situation. When you spend some time with someone who is homeless and hear their story, you might understand how close many of us are to falling over that edge. When you travel to other places and see how people live, a deep desire for a better life, no matter what the cost is, makes more sense.

Connection breeds kindness. Understanding brings kindness. My wish is for people to all show a little more kindness. Here are some ways you can inject some kindness into the world:

- Share your bounty of vegetables.
- Make eye contact with that homeless person sitting on the corner.
- Have some sympathy for those facing terrible choices or having their children ripped out of their arms.
- Speak up for someone who doesn't have a voice.
- Use someone's preferred pronoun, even if you don't understand what the fuss is about.
- Let someone cut ahead of you when you are driving, even if they don't seem to understand how to do a zipper merge.
- Believe that people experience racism, even if you don't see it yourself. And ask yourself how you can use your privilege to help.
- Mentor someone at your work.
- Believe a woman who tells you she was sexually assaulted.
- Hold the door for people coming in behind you.
- Assume that people have good intentions and meet them where they are with love and respect.
- Don't engage with the person you disagree with on social media.
- Pay for the coffee of the person in line behind you.
- Let the lady with three items go ahead of you at the grocery store.
- Smile.

We all want kindness for ourselves. Sometimes the best way to receive kindness is to give it

---

Reflection Questions:

- *When's the last time someone did something nice for you without expecting anything in return? How did it feel?*
- *Name three things you can do today to offer kindness to someone*

else.

Keeping It Together When You're Pulled in Too Many Directions

Why a Toy from My Childhood is a Quarantine Metaphor — And What to Do About It

This pandemic has us being pulled in so many directions that some of us feel like we're at the breaking point.

It reminds me of this time two excited dogs tried to rip me in half.

My roommate was out of town, so I brought her dog along for a walk with me and my dog. As I wandered through the neighborhood with a hyper dog on each side, I felt a new appreciation for dog walkers. Apparently if they walk together, both dogs totally forget that they know how to heel and walk nicely.

We stopped in the nearby vacant lot where all the best grass grows so the dogs could have a little grassy snack. All of a sudden, as if they had planned it, both dogs took off like a shot in opposite directions.

They each quickly reached the end of their leashes and began to pull hard on my arms, and for a moment I felt like Stretch Armstrong.

Like Stretch Armstrong, my arms lengthened but didn't pop off — although it felt iffy for a moment.

I realized it's a good metaphor for life. How many times do we feel like we are being pulled in different directions? And then we wonder, is this going to break me?

The good news is, no, it's not going to break you. But you do need to find a way to reduce the tension.

But here are some tips for when you are feeling overwhelmed with too many competing priorities:

- *Take a breath.* Sometimes the best thing you can do when you're feeling overwhelmed is to stop for a moment and take a breath[1]. Just stop moving and listen to your breath. Try deepening it or slowing it down. Bring your awareness into your body and let oxygen fill your cells. It works.
- *Cut Yourself Some Slack.* Look, it's a once-in-a-century pandemic. It's hard. You may not be able to focus on your work as closely when your cat is walking over your keyboard and your kid is asking for help with fractions. We're all doing the best we can. Your house may not be as clean as you prefer, and you may not be learning how to bake sourdough bread and that's OK. There's time for all that later, when life goes back to normal.
- *Make a list and prioritize.* It can help to just go over everything that you've got going on and figure out what can wait. Write it on a piece of paper or use an app on your phone. Ask yourself, do I really need to do this? If so, does it need to be today? What will happen if I put this off for later? If I can't do everything, what's most crucial right now? Make a list and knock off the urgent or quick items first.
- *Focus.* If you're like me, sometimes at your most overwhelmed you'll think, "Let me just check Facebook before I get started", or "Oh look, the Golden Girls is on" (don't judge me, Golden Girls is a classic). There are times when it's great to take a break, and then are times when you're wasting time and increasing your stress as your to-do list sits there, untouched. I often will tell myself that I'm going to

---

1. http://rosebakenterprises.com/2018/08/15/the-importance-of-taking-a-breath/

totally focus and work on my list for 30 minutes and then I can stop. Sometimes I stop after 30 minutes, sometimes I get on a roll and keep going, but either way, I always feel better if I spend some focused time getting things done.

- *Learn how to say no.* This can be really difficult, especially for those of us who identify as women and have been socialized to be people-pleasers, but sometimes you just need to learn to say no. The fact is, some people will take advantage of your helpful nature. Some people suck the life out of you. And some people can do fine all on their own if you let them. Before you agree to join one more committee or take on one more project at work or be the person who takes your kid to their dance lessons while your partner watches tv, think about saying no. Allow others to step up. Be assertive when you need help. And prioritize those activities that are most important to you.

- *Remember you always have a choice.* Years ago when I was in therapy, I was complaining to my counselor about a work training that was very triggering and contentious. "What if you just don't go?" she asked me. "I don't have a choice, I have to go, it's mandatory", I answered. I'll never forget her response: "You always have a choice. Your choice is to go to the training and be upset, or not go to the training and be reprimanded by your boss. The problem isn't that you don't have a choice, the problem is you don't like your choices." When you remember that you're making a choice, even if it's choosing the lesser of two evils, it brings the control back to you.

- *Recharge.* You've heard the old saying, "You can't pour from an empty cup". No matter how long your to-do list is and how many commitments you have, you need to practice self-care. If your response to this is, "I don't have time for self-care" then you need it more than most. Do something that recharges you at least once a week. Practice yoga or meditation. Take a walk in the woods. Have dinner with low-maintenance friends. Play with your dog. Get a massage. We all have different things that make us happy and give us joy. Find that joy. I guarantee you that you can find an hour or two (hopefully more) in your life somewhere this week to focus on you. You'll be glad you did.

What are your favorite strategies for feeling less like Stretch Armstrong and more like you?

Reflection Questions:

- *What happens in your body when you're feeling stretched in too many directions? What makes it feel better?*
- *How often are you stretched too far because you can't say no? When did you say "no" to something and have it work out OK? How did you feel?*

We All Need the Human Touch

How Physical Connection Helps Us Relax

"We all need the human touch. We all need it, and I need it too!" — *Rick Springfield*

It's a pretty well-known fact that gentle human touch releases "feel good" hormones in our brains. (A lesser-known fact: listening to Rick Springfield releases "feel good" hormones in my own brain.)

I was dreaming about pre-quarantine days when I was free to get a massage. In my mind's eye I could imagine the massage and the way it always releases all kinds of feel good hormones in my brain .

Then I remembered something I heard once in a mindfulness meditation class: the instructor said that the body can't differentiate where touch comes from. She said that holding one of your hands with the other will have the same positive impact on your body as it would if someone else was holding your hand.

As I stretched my achy muscles and spaced out on a Zoom call, I pondered our need for touch. Having a massage, the touch of someone's hands, for most of us the experience feels healing. It helps us relax.

But it's not just massage that does this. Holding someone's hand, a hug, a touch on the shoulder — there are lots of ways we can increase connection with our fellow humans.

It's amazing how much we can communicate to each other with a simple touch. A pat on the back might convey a "good job" message. A gentle hand on an arm shows support or comfort to someone without a word. A few months ago, I was in a meeting with a coworker and she touched her foot against mine when something happened. I knew it was her way of silently saying, "Can you believe this?"

Touch can also be a self-soothing activity. We rub our stomachs when they hurt. We rub our hands together when we are cold. And massaging an ear or a temple can help reduce pain or cravings.

Researchers have determined that touch has many benefits including:

- Reducing stress or anxiety
- Encouraging positive thinking
- Boosting immune system
- Lowering blood pressure
- Showing empathy
- Promoting trust and connection
- Improving communication

The desire to touch is instinctual. If a friend is having a hard time I might offer her a hug. Although I'm not a person who normally likes to hug, I had the reflex to hug her and try to make her feel better.

Touch between species can also be beneficial for both parties. I once had a very empathic dog, and whenever I was sad or stressed, she would come lay her head in my lap to offer comfort. Rubbing your dog's head or petting your cat's back will relax the animal, and probably you as well. Animals are widely used in a variety of therapeutic interventions for humans.

In this world of social distancing and working from home, many of us are craving that human connection more than ever. How do we ensure that we get the benefits of touch?

Start with yourself. Hold your hand over your heart for a moment, close your eyes and focus on the rhythm of your heart. Give yourself a little self-massage, gently and slowly rubbing your hands over your arms, legs, shoulders, neck, while imagining your breath moving towards any area that feels tight or sore.

Then expand your focus to family, friends, and the people you live with. Oftentimes we come and go without really "seeing" the people around us. Put down your phone, turn off the TV and interact with those around you. Give them a hug. Touch their arm while you talk to them. Rub their back or their head. Hold their hand. Go with your instincts and see what feels good for both of you.

It doesn't have to be long and you don't have to make a big deal of it. Adding small touches and points of human contact throughout the day will all add up to increased connection and well-being for you and those around you. Add some touch to your life today. You'll be happy you did.

Reflection Questions:

- *When's the last time you felt the loving touch of another person? How did it feel in your body? In your mind?*
- *How can you add more touch into your life?*

You Need to Create Your Own Family

The family you make is often better than the family you were born with

I got home from work one night and sat on my bed to check e-mail. In walks the cat, then a roommate, then a dog, then another roommate, then another dog, and before I knew it the whole family was sitting on my bed. All six of us, which no doubt tested the limits of my bed frame.

As we talked about our day, I looked around and felt a surge of gratitude[1]. I thought to myself, my family is pretty damn awesome.

Some of us have awesome families that they're born into, and some of us have awesome families that we create. Like many people, I've created my own family. It's a blend of someone I'm related to by blood (my sister), someone I'm not related to (my best friend) and a hodgepodge of neurotic animals.

The three of us (six if you count the animals) live together in the same house and have done so for several years. We have ongoing daily group texts. We generally eat dinner together. We split up the household chores. We share the shopping.

We all have our own separate lives and separate spaces and separate friends, but we also do some things together. We tease each other. We make big decisions together. We give each other emotional support. We share responsibility for the animals. We laugh.

Each of us contributes to the household and the family in our own significant way. We are all smart and cool and independent. We are each very different, yet we have a lot in common. It works very well for us.

---

1. https://rosebak.medium.com/how-cultivating-gratitude-is-changing-my-perspective-on-life-5fb5eb1f0e13

Some people think it's weird that there are three adult women living together in our house, but I like to think of us as the middle-aged version of the Golden Girls[2]. Except we don't wear shoulder pads. I'm Dorothy of course.

People have different reasons for creating families. Some of the most common include: their birth family is toxic or abusive[3], they've been rejected by a family who can't accept them for who they are[4], they live too far away from family, their family is dead, or they were raised in foster care.

But the fact is, the "traditional" family isn't the norm anymore for many of us. And you know what? That's OK because where your bio family may be lacking, you have the ability to create a family that is healthy and works for you.

Creating a family is empowering. It's a gift to choose to surround yourself with people who unconditionally love and support you. So who's your family?

Think about things like:

- Who is there for you when things are rough?
- Who do you list as your emergency contact?
- Who do you call when something exciting happens?
- Who do you trust with your kids or pets?
- Who puts up with you when you're crying or depressed or annoying or cranky?
- Who likes you just for you, not for who they want you to be?
- Who can you have an issue with, and talk through it?

---

2. https://en.wikipedia.org/wiki/The_Golden_Girls

3. https://medium.com/illumination/why-its-ok-to-divorce-your-family-776bf2d91086

4. https://rosebak.medium.com/when-family-holidays-are-more-horror-than-hallmark-d6069496c5a

- Who do you really want to spend holidays with?
- Which relationships are easy and mostly drama free?

The people who like you for who you are, the people who will be there for you when something goes wrong, the people who don't judge you, the people who love you unconditionally — those are your family, whoever they are. Embrace them. Celebrate their awesomeness. And if you can all live in a big old house together, even better.

Reflection Questions:

- *Who do you consider yourself to be close to? Are they family, friends, or both?*
- *If you were an orphan, who in your life right now would you consider family? What about your relationship with them makes them more than just friends?*

My Dog Got Hit by a Car and I Felt Lucky

How Cultivating Gratitude is Changing My Perspective on Life

I've been thinking a lot about gratitude the last few months. It started, as many good things do, as part of my yoga practice.

Although I've read a lot about cultivating gratitude I hadn't really given it much serious thought — it seemed kind of trendy and forced, like when you're at Thanksgiving and someone wants to go around the table and say why you're thankful.

But one day recently my yoga teacher spoke about gratitude in a way that really resonated with me. I opened my mind to it, and I've been consciously expressing gratitude ever since.

This is a big shift for me as I've lived most of my life as a bit of a pessimist. Not a full-on Eeyore, but definitely pragmatic. If something good happened, I figured it was only a matter of time before something bad happened to balance it out. People would be surprised I wasn't excited about a trip or a big event, and it because I was waiting to make sure it really happened. I bought a house and worried incessantly about how much work it was and what I'd do if something went wrong.

Years ago I was in therapy, and the therapist asked if I ever thought about killing myself. My response: I'm too pessimistic to kill myself, because it probably wouldn't work anyway. And I was totally serious.

For me, looking on the bright side and appreciating the good instead of focusing on the bad has been a huge shift in mindset.

There's been a lot of research on gratitude. Countless studies have shown that people who regularly identify the things they're grateful for and express gratitude have better mental and physical health, decreased stress and aggression, better resilience and an improved quality of life.

As I've thought about gratitude, I'm realizing it's more than just saying "thank you". It's about showing appreciation, showing love and showing kindness.

Saying "thank you" has become so reflexive that it often means nothing anymore. The cashier hands you change, you say thank you. Someone tells you that you look nice, you say thank you. Someone holds the door, you say thank you. It's a habit, like saying "have a nice day", but there's no real intention behind it.

Expressing gratitude has the extra element of reflecting on the "why" behind saying you're thankful and appreciating the thing you're thankful for.

You are grateful that the cashier is there providing service and giving you the correct change. You appreciate that someone noticed you and took the time to give you a compliment and the warm feelings the compliment generated. You acknowledge that someone took an extra couple seconds to hold the door instead of letting it slam in your face. It also shows a kindness to the person by demonstrating that you truly recognize what they did, even if it was something small.

It's a subtle shift, but a shift nonetheless. And the more I do it, the more positive my outlook becomes.

I read somewhere that you should identify three things you're grateful for every single day.

One day I was stuck in traffic, and I was feeling irritated about how long it was taking me to get to work. I turned off the news and decided to do the gratitude exercise. I said to myself, "I'm grateful that I have a job to go to and it's a job I love. I'm grateful that I have a car and money for gas and I'm not stuck on a hot bus in this traffic. I'm grateful that I live in a country where women can work outside the home and drive." I felt my irritation slipping away.

My situation hadn't changed, but my response to it had.

As a supervisor, I try to thank my staff for their work regularly. But now I'm actively trying to express gratitude instead. For example, instead of saying, "thank you for getting that report to me" I said, "I'm grateful that you did such a great job on this report and made sure it was on time."

At a team retreat I stated I was grateful for everyone's contributions and their commitment to the work instead of a meaningless "thanks for coming today".

In doing annual performance evaluations, I listed at least one accomplishment for each person and told them in detail why I was grateful for it. It was more meaningful for me to reflect on why I was grateful and to express my gratitude with kindness towards my team, and I hope it was meaningful for them as well.

A while back my dog was hit by a car. If it had happened six months earlier, I would have been ranting and annoyed for weeks. But instead, I reflected on the situation, and I consciously expressed gratitude. It really helped reduce my stress around what happened.

I told myself I'm grateful I was nearby when it happened and could get the dog right to the vet before he lost too much blood. I'm grateful that when I saw the enormous vet bill, I had funds available to get him the care he needed. I'm grateful he wasn't injured worse. I'm grateful the family friend who was walking him wasn't hit too.

It's still a really crappy thing that happened, but by focusing on the positives instead of the negatives, I'm not dwelling on it or pondering the "what ifs".

The more I cultivate gratitude in myself, the more grateful I become each day. And the more grateful I become, the calmer and happier I become. I know, this might sound a little woo-woo for some of you, but you might try it and see if it helps you as much as it has helped me.

I was a skeptic, but it really works.

I'm grateful that my yoga teacher shared this gift with me.

I'll end with this quote from the Dalai Lama that I love: "Every day, think as you wake up: Today I am fortunate to have woken up. I am alive. I have a precious human life. I am not going to waste it. I am going to use all my energies to develop myself, to expand my heart out to others, to achieve enlightenment for the benefit of all beings. I am going to have kind thoughts towards others, I am not going to get angry, or think badly about others. I am going to benefit others as much as I can."

Reflection Questions:

- *What do you do in your everyday life to create a benefit to others?*
- *How often do you think negative or judgmental thoughts? What can you do to interrupt these feelings when they occur?*

How to Stop Hating Yourself

It's Time to Join the Self-Love Revolution

"You have been criticizing yourself for years, and it hasn't worked. Try approving of yourself and see what happens."

— Louise L. Hay

I've been doing a lot of self-reflection since I turned 50. One of the things I've been focused on a lot is my longest and most important relationship — the relationship I have with myself.

Someone on Facebook posted something recently about wishing they could be back in the 80s and I responded that I only wish I were as "fat" now as I thought I was back then.

It was a joking reference to how many of us go through life so focused on our appearance that we don't appreciate how good we look until it's too late.

But as I reflected more on that off-hand comment, I became troubled. Clearly somewhere in my mind the 1980s me is better than 2018 me. Or better looking anyway. But why is that? Why would I turn that negativity inward? What if instead I believed I was beautiful then, and beautiful now too? Both can be true.

A teacher from the yoga studio where I practice summed up their teaching philosophy like this, "We approach everyone with the belief that they are perfect just as they are. I'm perfect, you're perfect, just as you are. You don't need to be fixed."

This is revolutionary. Seriously revolutionary.

I am perfect just the way I am. And so are you.

Think about how different things would be if we all believed that. There are literally millions of self-improvement books out there, many of which claim that loving yourself means changing yourself. Love yourself thin. Love yourself to heal disease. Love yourself to be get what you want. Love yourself to find a relationship. What do they have in common? The premise that to change yourself is an act of love.

It's very different from this idea that you should love yourself right now, just the way you are. It's the opposite of the belief that you should love yourself without the assumption that you are flawed and need to change something in order to move towards perfection.

Lately I've been engaging in a Buddhist practice called metta, or lovingkindness. I am no expert in Buddhism and am sure I'm missing the nuances, but the basic idea is that you send love and compassion out to the world, not just to those you already love, but to those you don't love, and those you don't know. And you also bring that love and compassion inward and focus it on yourself as well. I'm thinking about this practice often, in meditation, in yoga, and in my daily life and interactions with others.

For me it's much easier to send love out than to send love inward. It feels like some level of conceit or narcissism to say you love yourself, to say you're perfect. But it's so powerful.

As I've been consciously sending love and compassion to myself, I've been startled by the contrast between lovingkindness towards self and my previous state of mind.

And by "startled" I mean shocked and appalled. Honestly, I didn't know how many negative thoughts I had about myself until I started this practice. It's astounding.

If I were to say to others even 1% of the mean things I say to myself on a daily basis I would have no friends. My family would abandon me. Even my dog would hate me. It's so hardwired in my brain to criticize myself that I wasn't even aware of this ongoing loop of negativity playing at the edge of my thoughts like some kind of evil elevator music.

A method I've found particularly helpful to get this loop of self-criticism is the use of the word "neti", which is Sanskrit for "not this". It's a way to counteract the negative thoughts each of us have every day. Instead of just observing your thoughts, like a lot of meditation techniques teach, you actually counteract them. You push that negative thought away and don't give it any power or attention.

So when something negative pops in my head, like when I looked down at my legs in yoga class and thought, "Gross, I shouldn't be wearing shorts, I forgot to shave my legs", I counteract it by saying firmly in my head, "neti, neti".

When I look at someone and think, "I wish I were as young and thin and beautiful as her" I now say to myself "neti, neti, I'm perfect the way I am."

Recently I heard someone say, "I'm perfect" and another person chuckled, like many would, as if it was a joke. "I'm serious", the person responded. And she was. Before I embarked on this journey I would have chuckled as well. Instead I thought with admiration, "Good for her. She's right, she is perfect just as she is. We all are."

Today I challenge you to do something revolutionary. I challenge you to love yourself. You're perfect just the way you are. And so am I.

Reflection Questions:

- *Close your eyes and trace the shape of your body in your imagination. Notice the curves and angles. What part of your body feels the most beautiful?*

- *Think of a time your body worked well for you. What body parts are the strongest? What are the most flexible?*

What Dogs Can Teach Us About Joy

What if we were better at finding joy in the mundane?

My dog Edison was due for a physical and vaccinations recently, so we headed to the vet. Edison is, in my unbiased opinion, the cutest dog ever.

He's large and goofy with white fur and black spots. He has deep soulful eyes. He also has the funniest ears, very expressive, and usually one is lying on his head while the other is popped out like an old antenna searching for a signal.

Sadly those ears don't actually work, so we've taught Edison doggy sign language.

When I take him for a walk, random strangers stop their cars to tell me how cute he is. Everyone is his friend. He even has his own Instagram account.

Edison is very exuberant and finds joy in everything we do. When Edison is happy he vibrates with joy. He wags his tail so hard his whole butt moves with him. And when he smiles, it's a thing of beauty.

We get into the car to go to the vet and, oh my god, we're going for a ride, it's the best thing ever! Then we get to the vet and people are oohing and ahhing and petting him and it's the best thing ever! The vet tech gave him a treat of liver spread on a pretzel, and it was the best thing ever! We came home and took a nice long walk and... well, you get the idea.

Seeing Edison's joy in something as mundane as going to the vet made me reflect on how dogs seem to find joy in everything. A pat on the head, a piece of jerky as a treat, a game of tug of war, me coming home from work, a walk, seeing his best friend Buddy... it's all very joyful for Edison.

As adults we don't pay attention to these little things, and we lack the joyful enthusiasm we had as children. But dogs never seem to lose their sense of joy.

I might be happy to see my best friend, but I am not overwhelmed with excitement the way Edison is when he sees someone he loves.

If I have a treat I might think, this is good, but I don't take the time or the effort to take joy in the taste of the treat or how it makes me feel. Edison does: He has some treats he will savor all day.

I'm never excited about going to the doctor. I never roll around in the grass. And I never stick my head out the window to feel the breeze when I'm in the car.

But what if I did? What if we found joy in the mundane? What if we were joyous for everything we were given? How would our attitude change if we looked for the joy in the little things of everyday life?

Today I resolve to be more joyful. To take pleasure in the simple things. To be in the moment and embrace the experience. Today I resolve to experience joy like a dog named Edison.

Reflection Questions:

- *Name five things that give you joy, no matter how small.*
- *Close your eyes and focus on the word "joy". What things float into your mind? Why are these things associated with joy for you?*

When Sibling Rivalry Fades & You Find New Friends

How to Cultivate Rewarding Adult Friendships with Your Brothers and Sisters

Your siblings are likely among your longest relationships.

If you grew up with siblings, you know that these relationships can be complicated. You share a history, you know where the skeletons are buried in the family closet, and you know how to make each other feel good, or how to push each other's buttons.

Growing up, your siblings might have been your best friends or your worst enemies. Probably for most people, this depended on the sibling. But generally, one of the most rewarding things can be an adult relationship with your brothers and sisters, in whatever way works for you.

So how do you cultivate a healthy(ish) adult relationship with the sibs?

First, I just want to acknowledge that for some of us, there is one or more sibling relationship that is so toxic it's best to have little or no contact with them. As they say, you do you. Don't force a relationship with someone who is abusive or has damaged the relationship beyond repair.

For the rest of the sibling gamut, here are a few things to consider if you'd like to interact with your siblings in a healthier manner as an adult.

Break out of your childhood roles

The first thing to be aware of is that many of us tend to re-enact our childhood roles even as adults. This includes acting in our assigned roles: the brat, the smart one, the pretty one, the troublemaker, the bossy one, the baby, etc.

For example, I'm the oldest and served in a parental role towards my siblings. Even though my youngest sibling is 40, I still find myself assuming leadership of the sibs when we are together. And what I call "assuming leadership" my siblings call "being bossy".

They're wrong of course, because I'm always right, but I'm willing to hear their feedback. This results in conversations like this:

Me: "Be careful, get away from there!"

Sibling: "I'm 40 years old, not 5. I can assess the danger of standing here all by myself now."

Me: "You're going downtown? Do you know where you're going?"

Sibling: "I think I can figure out how to use MapQuest by now."

Me: "Did you wash your hands?"

Sibling: (huge sigh and eye roll as they walk away)

Get over childhood hurts

I get it, no matter how close you were to your sibs growing up, there was probably something terrible that happened. An injury. A cherished possession ruined. Someone blames someone else for what they actually did. A feeling that a parent liked one sibling more than the other. A stolen boyfriend. Normal sibling conflict.

Either let it go or talk it out. Do you really want to hold a grudge for something that happened 30 years ago? Why continue to blame people for something they did when their brains weren't fully formed?

Seriously, remember how stupid you acted when you were a kid? Do you want to be held accountable for that now?

My siblings and I mostly tease each other about that stuff these days, like "remember that time you hit me in the face with a cup?" or "remember that time you scammed each of your sisters out of money?" or "remember when I ran you over with the car?" (That last one's a joke by the way).

Keep in Touch

Try to maintain regular contact with your sibs so you not only have that connection but know what's going on in each other's lives. Try things like regular phone calls or group texts. Call each other for your birthdays (Not good with dates? Use a calendar — there's one right there in your phone.).

If talking or seeing each other live feels difficult, embrace technology like e-mail and texts. It's a good way to communicate, especially if you have sibs who are prone to hurt feelings or easily offended in live interactions.

In addition to direct conversations, my sibs and I have a running group text. We usually text our little group several times a week with news, jokes, pictures, and other things that catch our interest. And I individually text with my sibs almost daily. That may be more than you want to interact but try to check in at least once a week if possible.

And also, be sure to celebrate milestones like a promotion or a major birthday or a completed half marathon. Celebrate your siblings!

Create a group challenge or virtual group activity

Depending on the relationship you have, sometimes it's fun to do a little challenge that will have you checking in regularly, like a "plank a day" challenge, or dissecting the latest episode of your favorite TV show. A quick conversation like, "I ran my 2 miles today" can lead to more significant communication and building connection.

Get a family tattoo

On a recent trip to Hawaii to celebrate my 50th birthday, we all got tattoos with a symbol for "perseverance and decided that would be our sibling motto. Now every time I see my tattoo, I think of my sibs.

Set aside some dedicated sibling time

Regardless of whether you live close or far away, try to carve out some "sibling only" time, either one on one or in a group, or ideally both. I know there are times when it's fun to get all the significant others and kids together, like on Christmas for example, but make some time to create an adult relationship with the sibs that's separate from your individual families.

Many years ago my sibs and I implemented "Brother-Sister Weekend". At least once a year I get together with both my siblings who I still have a relationship with, and we do something that's just the three of us.

We often go to a sporting event, like a Chicago Bears football game, or an event, like running a half marathon in Las Vegas. Sometimes we do something at a beach somewhere. In our downtime we usually binge watch movies or episodes of "My Name is Earl", eat way too much junk food, and tell crazy stories about our dead parents or stuff we remember from childhood. And we have serious conversations too.

The important thing is it's a time to have an adult relationship with each other. You don't have to be BFFs with your sibs, but you can definitely be friends.

Reflection Questions:

- *Which siblings (if any) are you closest with? Why or why not? Has it changed over the years?*
- *What does an ideal relationship with your siblings look like for you? Are there steps you can take to move in that direction?*

Why It's OK to Divorce Your Family

How to decide if it's time to break ties with your family members

We all have our own ideas of the "perfect family". Maybe it's the Cleavers or the Bradys or the Father Knows Best family (am I aging myself here?).

The reality of it is, most of our families don't measure up to those impossible standards.

Family can be difficult, we all get that. Some family relationships take a lot of work, or a lot of gritting your teeth, or a lot of self-care to navigate. But sometimes you have a family relationship that is beyond repair.[1]

Maybe it's a parent with severe alcoholism or a sibling with mental illness. Maybe it's a family member who has done something so awful, there's no coming back from that. What do you do then?

Sometimes your best option is to sever the relationship and divorce your family member.

For many of us, this can be one of the hardest decisions we ever make. It comes with judgment from all sides.

You may hear things like "It's terrible that your father abused you, but I'm sure he loves you in his own way", or "No matter what your mom did, she's old now and you owe it to her to help her out", or "Your daughter has a drug problem, but you're still her mom".

---

1. https://rosebak.medium.com/when-family-holidays-are-more-horror-than-hallmark-d6069496c5a

Here's the thing: no one will take care of *you* in these abusive family relationships.

You need to take care of yourself, and sometimes taking care of yourself means removing yourself from that situation. You don't have to forgive huge, horrible things that came in your past and you certainly don't have to put up with ongoing abuse.

You deserve to live your best life, even if it means cutting people off.

I know it sounds simple, but it is not. Family bonds are usually our oldest and strongest bonds. They are also nuanced and complicated.

Here are some things to consider before divorcing a family member:

- Is the family member abusive in all your interactions? Or is abuse brought on by triggers such as drugs or alcohol? Are there ways to maintain some level of the relationship while avoiding exposing yourself to abuse?
- Are you willing or able to forgive past abuse? Or do you find yourself angry, hurt, or reliving past deeds whenever you see the person?
- Does the person take responsibility for their behavior? Have they asked for forgiveness, changed in some tangible way, or made amends?
- How will this impact other members of your immediate family? For example, do you feel like another person will feel forced to choose between you and your estranged family member? Does severing the relationship mean your kids won't see a grandparent or aunt, and if so, are you OK with that?
- When the person dies, what do you think you will feel? Regret that you stopped having a relationship with that person? Relief? Or will you mourn that you didn't have a

different family member?

- If you never see or talk to the person again, will you be OK with it?
- Do you have a strong support system to get you through this? Sometimes friends can be the family you need.

Only you can decide if ending the relationship is best for you. If you make the difficult decision to end the relationship, be sure to take care of yourself.

And remember, it's totally OK to not respond to calls, emails, or other attempts from the family member to engage with you. Once you've told them it's over, you have no obligation to engage.

It's OK to change the subject and agree to disagree with well-meaning friends or family that want to tell you why you should maintain the relationship.

If you feel like the person poses a current danger to you, contact your local family violence agency, court, or an attorney to determine your options for protective orders (restraining orders) if appropriate.

Most importantly, allow yourself space and time to mourn the relationship.

Practice self-care. Cry if you need to. Write in a journal or write a letter to the person (even if you don't send it) sharing your feelings. Talk to trusted family or friends who will understand.

Give yourself credit for taking care of yourself in a way that works best for you.

It can be helpful to have a neutral person talk this through, offer suggestions, and reinforce that you deserve to live a life free of abuse. If the relationship or end of the relationship is making you consider self-harm, or interfering with your daily activities, contact your local mental health agency or a therapist immediately.

Remember, you were born into your family — the decision to stay is completely up to you.

Reflection Questions:

- *Are there people in your family that you have a toxic relationship with? Do you get anything positive out of spending time with that person? Ask yourself honestly: is the relationship worth saving?*
- *If you never saw your toxic family member again, how would you feel? Why?*

Quit Wasting Valuable Time in the Shower

119

How to Make Your Shower Time More Productive and Start Your Day Off on a Happy Note

The average person spends 8.2 minutes in the shower.

That's almost an hour a week if you shower every day. If you are just using your shower time to space out while you wash your body, you're squandering a golden opportunity to multi-task.

There are many things that you can do in the shower to help use your time more wisely. Here are some great activities you can do in the shower and use your time more effectively:

Meditation

The shower is a great time to meditate. You're alone. It's probably quiet, other than the soothing sound of the running water. The steam creates a bit of a hazy effect that's perfect to help you to move your mind to a receptive state.

How to do it: Focus on your breath as you move through your shower routine. Concentrate on feeling the sensation of the washcloth rubbing on your body, or your fingers massaging your scalp. When your mind wanders, bring it back to your breath, or the feeling of your hands on your body. You may even want to choose a mantra to repeat with each breath.

Oil Pulling

The ancient Ayurvedic practice of oil pulling is believed to pull toxins from your body, whiten your teeth, freshen your breath, and reduce gum disease. Some believe it also has an anti-inflammatory effect on your body.

How to do it: Before you get into the shower, get about one tablespoon of coconut, sesame seed, or olive oil. Put it in your mouth and swish it around your mouth, forcing it around your teeth and gums while being careful not to swallow it. When you're done with your shower, spit it out into the trash can — not the sink or toilet — to avoid clogging the pipes. Rinse your mouth with water and enjoy the fresh feeling in your mouth.

Learn a New Language

Use your 8 minutes to listen and repeat some language lessons. You'll learn a useful skill and keep your mind engaged. Even listening to lessons a few short minutes each day will help you improve your skills.

How to do it: Download a language app on one of your devices. Be sure to keep the device away from water and steam as much as possible. You may want to use wireless speakers designed for the bathroom. When you enter the bathroom, start your lesson, and listen while you brush your teeth, shower, and get ready. You'll feel smarter by the time you are done.

Plan Your Day and Manifest Success

There's a technique in Law of Attraction called "segment intending". In the simplest terms, segment intending is when you set your intention for what's coming next. When you consciously visualize what will happen as if it has already occurred, you will create that reality.

How to do it: Close your eyes or soften your gaze and imagine the next part of your day. Let's say it's going to work. Visualize that you get dressed, and you feel good about how you look. You get into the car and it starts right away. Traffic is lighter than usual, and you easily find parking near your office. Imagine how you'll feel when you get into the office and all these things have come to pass. Use your imagination — it will help you manifest what you want.

Give Yourself a Facial

With the steam opening up your pores, shower time can be a great opportunity to also give your skin some TLC. The addition of an exfoliating scrub or a healing mask can help you look younger and fresher by the time you're done.

How to do it: Find a great face mask or exfoliating scrub that is non-comedogenic and works with your skin. You may want to use something like a clay or mud mask, or a papaya or charcoal scrub. Apply it to your face and neck with soothing upward strokes and let it rest on your face while you wash your body.

When you're finished cleaning up, use the warm shower water to gently remove the remnants of the treatment, then pat your face dry with a towel. Be sure to moisturize afterward to keep your skin hydrated.

Sing Your Heart Out

If all else fails, at least sing while you're in the shower. Numerous studies have shown that singing can lower cortisol levels (your stress hormones), exercise your lungs, elevate your mood, and even reduce pain by increasing oxytocin levels ("the love hormone").

How to do it: You know this one. Just think of a song that makes you happy, and belt it out. Don't worry if you don't know the words — you can make them up and no one will know the difference. If you get stuck, try one of these ideas: "Dancing Queen" by Abba, "Don't Stop Believing" by Journey, "I Got a Feeling" by the Black Eyed Peas, or make like Kermit and sing "Rainbow Connection".

Reflection Questions:

- *How do you react when you think about taking "dead time" like a shower and using the time differently? Why?*
- *What other activities can you do during the shower, or while waiting in line, or other times when you're not actively engaged in something?*

You Deserve a Total Bed Make-Over

Ten Ways that Replacing Your Sheets and Pillows Will Improve Your Life

"I can't sleep any more. It's too much like death." — Cosmo Castorini in "Moonstruck"

We are all spending most of our time at home these days so I have to ask you: when's the last time you replaced your pillows, bought new sheets or updated your bedspread?

I was in bed the other night, tossing and turning, when I had the sudden urge to use the restroom. Apparently when you hit your 50s, your nights become an endless series of bathroom trips.

Anyway, I looked down and realized I had my pillows folded over and bunched up like a bunch of rags. Frowning, I shook them out a bit and took a good look at them. My pillows were flat, misshapen, and old.

My sheets weren't much better. They were faded and threadbare. Those poor sheets have seen a lot of hot flashes and snuggling dogs (don't judge me). I have rags that look better than my sheets did.

I haven't slept well since 1980, but even so, I wondered how much worse my sleep was because of my ratty old bedding. I often find myself inexplicably itchy and with sore muscles from sleeping wrong on my pillows.

Why does my bed look like it belongs to a broke college student? I wondered.

I couldn't even remember the last time I replaced my bedding. In the past I have tended to just buy whatever is cheap and sturdy and keep it for a few years, or maybe a decade.

Honestly, I don't think about my bedding a lot.

When I do think about bedding, it's usually because I'm in a nice hotel with high thread-count sheets and high quality pillows. Then I'm thinking how great it'd be to have that at home until I go home and forget all about it.

That night, I resolved to treat myself to new bedding.

I decided to start with pillows. But how to choose? There are approximately a million pillows, so I made a mental list of things that were important to me, like suitable for side sleepers, chemical free, hypoallergenic, and not too hard or too soft. I wound up trying a few different types before I found pillows that are comfortable and supportive for my body.

Then I moved onto sheets. After some obsessive research I settled on some soft and stylish bamboo sheets that are both hypoallergenic and moisture wicking (hot flashes, remember?).

I got rid of any sheets, blankets or comforters that were ripped, faded, had a funky smell, or looked like they had followed me around since the 90s.

I didn't go crazy, but I also did not go cheap. I only purchased items that checked off everything on my list. Everything I bought had consistently good reviews, was sustainable and hypoallergenic, and was mid-range in price. Oh, and they had to be visually appealing.

When my new bedding arrived, I felt surprisingly excited. It felt kind of decadent, like I was really treating myself, except there was no chocolate or alcohol involved. It made me wonder why I hadn't bought new bedding a long time ago.

Experts say you should replace your pillows, sheets, and bedding after about two years of use. An upgrade of your bedding has several important benefits, including:

It's an easy way to give your bedroom a decorating face lift, especially when you're home all the time

Improving sleep so you wake up more rested

Alleviating neck or shoulder issues from broken down pillows

Removing allergens like dust mites and dander

Stimulating the "feel good" hormones that flood your brain when you feel indulged

Reducing skin issues like acne, wrinkles, or rosacea

Minimizing night sweats or overheated sleeping

Protecting your mattress so it lasts longer

Supporting your head and neck may reduce snoring and sleep apnea

Counteracting the scarcity mindset that many of us start adulthood with — it feels good to move past the days of goodwill sheets and hand-me-down pillows

Tonight when I lay in bed, it'll be on my fluffy and comfortable new pillows and my soft and luxurious new sheets. I may even get a little bit of sleep — until I have to pee again.

Reflection Questions:

- *How much attention to you pay to your bed and your sleep hygiene? Why or why not?*
- *If you closed your eyes and imagined your perfect bedroom, what*

would it look like? What would it feel like? Can you incorporate those elements into your current bedroom?

Recovering from the Trauma of the Presidential Physical Fitness Test

What a Dead Gym Teacher, a Former President and Teaching Yoga Have Taught Me About Embracing Movement

My grade school gym teacher died recently.

When I saw the post on Facebook my first thought was, "Wow, it's been over thirty years since I was in grade school. I can't believe that woman was still alive."

My second thought was, "At least she won't torture anyone else."

With the perspective of adulthood, I can acknowledge that my gym teacher was likely a very nice person just doing her job, but to me she was the master of reign of terror that still scars me to this day.

Her co-conspirator: President John F. Kennedy.

I have a big grudge against JFK. My grandpa's rolling in his grave right now since JFK was our first and only Catholic president and therefore was, in Grandpa's eyes, perfect. But JFK was also responsible for the unique grammar school torture known as the Presidential Physical Fitness Test (PPFT).

If you went to grammar school (or if you didn't grow up in the Midwest, "grade" school) in the 1970s you know exactly what I'm talking about. Once a year we were subjected to a series of tests ostensibly designed to evaluate our stamina and strength. I think it also had something to do with keeping us fit enough to fight Russians too.

I don't remember all the components exactly but I know there were several including: pull-ups, some kind of thing involving running across the gym picking up an eraser and running back, a touching your toes flexibility test, a rope climb, and the worst part — mile run.

When I was a kid, I loved school. Back to School day was the best day of the year. I loved everything about school except for gym, which I hated with a fiery passion. But even regular gym class was a picnic next to the PPFT. I dreaded it all year. Even thinking about it now I want to throw up. It was the only time all year I tried to fake sickness and stay home, that's how much I hated it. I never faked being sick.

School in the 1970s wasn't like it was now. There were no anti-bullying campaigns, no tolerance for differences, no "everyone gets an award, so no one feels bad", and no political correctness. And unlike today where it appears a good portion of the kids are fat, there was only one fat kid in school — and that kid was me.

Grammar school was a freaking jungle where the strongest survived. A jungle where we had gym every day and gym involved getting hit on the head with dodge balls and being mocked for having no sports skills and being picked last for teams if you weren't athletic or popular.

It was completely impossible for me, the lone fat kid, the pass the stupid PPFT test. Every single other kid in class could run a mile and pass the test — except me.

I would try of course. I'd go out too fast trying to keep up, then all the other kids would drop me in a few yards. I remember the humiliation of being out of breath, wheezing, having to stop and walk the final few laps. The other kids would taunt me as I lurched towards the finish line, sweat pouring down my little red face, bent over with hands on my knees, trying not to cry. My gym teacher would sigh at me, telling me I was the only one who didn't pass and how it was making our school look bad. Every year the anxiety got worse.

I grew up in a family where no one was athletic. With a few exceptions no one did sports, honestly no one ever got off the couch unless it was to go to the refrigerator for a beer.

Instead of creating any interest in athletics, the trauma of the PPFT taught me to avoid activity, to fear it. It taught me that there was nothing worse than trying something active and failing because there will be a bunch of mean kids laughing at you while the teacher glares at you disapprovingly.

Those messages burned themselves into my brain. In adulthood as I've pursued various physical activities I've struggled with working out in front of others. It makes me anxious, as if somewhere in the deep recesses of my mind I actually think a bunch of adults are going to taunt me for being too slow or looking weird, which of course they are not. People mostly are too in their own heads to pay attention to me.

One of the best things I've done is become a yoga teacher. Standing in front of the class demonstrating poses has done wonders for my self-confidence. I don't look like the Instagram yoga teachers, and neither do most of my students, and that's OK.

Just like grammar school Rose, I keep trying, even if I am the slowest or the sweatiest or the least graceful. Because that's all you can do — try your best. Try your best to be active, to move your body, to feel good. Life's too short to do anything else.

Reflection Questions:

- *Are there thing from childhood that still traumatize you? How do these things come up and how do you recognize that?*
- *How does it feel to move your body? Is there shame or joy? Which physical activities feel best for your body?*

Let Peace Begin with Me

Inner Peace is More Than a Buzzword

"When you find peace within yourself, you become the kind of person who can live at peace with others." —Peace Pilgrim

I was in a yoga class earlier this week and the teacher led us in a guided meditation. "Imagine a time you were at peace with yourself," she began. "Remember how you felt then, what it was like to be at peace."

And I thought, "Huh? At peace with myself? When was I at peace with myself?" And I thought some more. The meditation ended. I thought some more. Class ended. I thought some more, days went by. And I have to conclude that I've never been at peace with myself.

"Is anyone ever at peace with themselves?" my roommate asked when I told her about this. Good question.

I started to reframe the meditation in my head. Maybe they were really asking you to think of a time you felt at peace and draw on that. Yet my roommate's question kept coming back to me. I'm assuming some people are at peace with themselves, but I'm guessing they are a minority.

I've never been totally at peace with myself. Or even close. As I reflected on the magnitude of that realization, I felt sad. It seems like I should be able to be at peace with myself, at least sometimes.

What would it look like if I was at peace with myself, I wondered? For one thing, that voice in my head who I think of as my inner critic would be silent. Just thinking about that voice being gone makes me feel more peaceful. Going through an entire day without that voice nagging me that I'm too fat, not getting enough accomplished, not eating the way I'm "supposed" to be, not attractive enough, not tidy enough, not.....whatever enough.

What if that voice were gone and I (gasp) just accepted myself as perfect and whole just the way I am? The way I strive to do with the people around me.

What if instead of rehashing the past or thinking about the future, things I have to do, things I want to do, things that may or may not happen, I just focus on the present? What if I let go of regrets and judgements and plans and focus on really knowing myself? The real me.

And not to go all Serenity Prayer on you, but what if instead of worrying about things I can't change, I accept that many things are out of my control, and focus on what I can actually impact?

I know there's no easy answer, but I'm committed to finding peace within myself. I'm a lot closer than I was in the past, this I know. Practicing gratitude, incorporating yoga and meditation, and letting go of toxic relationships have helped me immensely, particularly over the last year when I've really focused on these areas.

Now I'm ready to take the next step. Being at peace with myself. Who's with me?

Reflection Questions:

- *When do you feel most at peace? What makes you feel that way?*
- *What tools work for you to quiet a busy mind?*

How Falling on My Butt Helped Me Deal with My Fear

I was afraid I would be embarrassed working out, but it wasn't that bad after all.

Well after twenty-five years of worrying it finally happened: I fell on my butt in a group yoga class.

Don't worry, I wasn't hurt. We were going into an extremely low squat, where your butt is only a few inches above the ground, and the teacher suggested if it felt difficult to squat that low we should put blocks under us to take some of the weight. As I lowered into a deep squat my legs started to give out. As I started to go down, I somehow missed the blocks and fell on my butt. Oops.

Although it was embarrassing, it was an important opportunity for personal growth.

Let me tell you why this is significant: I have practiced yoga on and off for over twenty-five years now. Every time we do a balance pose or a deep lunge or a low squat I think to myself, "Holy crap, I hope I don't fall!" That twinge of anxiety ratchets up a bit if I get shaky, like if I'm doing a standing balance pose and I feel myself start to sway. I'll come out of the pose more quickly because I'm afraid I'll fall. I thought more about falling than I did about staying upright.

I' realized that I'm not particularly worried that I'll hurt myself if I fall, because honestly, in real life I trip and/or fall quite often. Once I was hiking with my ex-boyfriend (who was WAY less athletic than me) and I tripped on something, I'm pretty sure it was a leaf or an ant or something equally innocuous. He shook his head and said, "I swear, there can be a twig 10 feet away from you and you'll manage to trip on it."

My fear of falling in yoga is about one thing: the fear of being embarrassed.

I have spent a lot of my life either feeling embarrassed or being worried that I might be embarrassed. When I was doing a lot of running, I often felt embarrassed that I was slower and larger than the other runners — even though no one ever, not even once, did anything to make me feel embarrassed.

Same thing for things like barre class, spin class and other group workout activities. Yet the fear of potentially being embarrassed was sometimes crippling.

Later during the class when I went into shavasana (the rest pose at the end of yoga class) I thought about why I'm so afraid to embarrass myself in a workout. What was the big deal? What had I missed out on because I was afraid people would judge me?

I realized that, like much of my trauma, the fear of looking bad when I was doing something active stemmed from grammar school.

You all remember grammar school right? (This is also known as grade school or elementary school depending where you live). It started out fun with the collages and turkeys made from the outline of your hand and singing cute songs and nap time, but around 4th or 5th grade it becomes a real-life "Lord of the Flies".

The kids separate into factions and some of the kids find themselves on the bottom. Right at the bottom of the heap is all the perceived misfits. In my school it was the fat kid, the kid with the lazy eye, the kid with a growth disorder, the kid who had frequent seizures, the kid who smelled bad, and a couple of other assorted kids who were "different".

I was the fat kid in class. I was picked last for any sport. I was last in every single "contest" we had for the highly traumatic (for me, at least) President's Physical Fitness Challenge, much to the annoyance of the other kids, and the gym teacher. I was the kid who couldn't seem to catch the ball that came right to me. I never could hit a baseball. I couldn't touch my toes. I was the kid who everyone had to wait to finish when we did laps.

Gym class was where the new world order was most evident. My lack of athletic ability and physical fitness made me super popular in gym class, or as I thought of it, the 7th circle of hell.

As time went on, I became increasingly worried about embarrassing myself, and that made me more tentative and afraid to try, because trying just led to more mockery. Instead I tried to be invisible as much as I could, or come up with excuses to miss class altogether.

The best thing that happened to me in 8th grade was when I had back surgery to correct severe scoliosis, because it meant I was excused from gym class for most of the school year. That's right, a 12-hour surgery followed by an extremely painful 9-month recovery was better than getting a dodge ball whipped at my head in gym class while people made fun of me.

Fast forward to the day when I fell in yoga for the first time and.....nothing bad happened. I looked around, but most people didn't seem to notice I had fallen. No one was laughing at me. My friend Betty raised her eyebrows and gave me a good-natured smile — Betty has probably run thousands of miles with me and is very familiar with my klutziness. No one mocked me after class. Nothing bad happened because I fell. It was NO BIG DEAL.

Sure, if that had happened in grammar school, I would have gotten a different response. But in the adult world, we are mostly all focused on ourselves.

It was a strong wake-up call for me. Who care if I look different or have different abilities in yoga or any other fitness class? I have the same right to be there, to take up space, to enjoy the feeling of being active.

As I lay in shavasana I focused on releasing that old fear. I radiated compassion for myself, and for the little fat kid who was tormented in gym class. I gave myself kudos for continuing on my journey to stay active.

I expressed gratitude to my body for all the times it held me up in class without falling. And I promised myself that I would never let the fear of embarrassment keep me from enjoying movement.

I felt relieved. I felt calm. I felt hopeful. The one thing I did not feel was embarrassed. And that's awesome.

Reflection Questions:

- *What's the most embarrassing thing that ever happened to you when you were working out? What happened after?*
- *In what ways does fear of embarrassment hold you back in your daily life? Who are the people you think will judge you? Do you really care about them?*

The Perfection Resolution

Why New Year's Resolutions Aren't Helping You – at All

I'm going to say something that may surprise you: you are perfect just the way you are. Yes, YOU. You are perfect the way you are right now. And so am I.

It doesn't matter if your thighs jiggle or your hair is frizzy or you eat donuts for dinner or you're cranky until you have coffee or you can't touch your toes or the only exercise you do it looking for the remote. You're still perfect just the way you are.

Today my email and social media is clogged with ads for "the best diet" and "special offers" for gyms and people I know starting "accountability groups" or offering to share their exciting new plan. Over and over again I've seen the phrase, "this is the year I'm going to finally (insert a resolution here)". And you know what? It all makes me sad.

People have been making New Year's resolutions for about 4,000 years, since back when the new year started in March. Ancient Babylonians started making resolutions at the new year to get in the good graces of the gods.

When Caesar implemented a new calendar system, the one that's the basis for today's calendar, he decreed that the New Year would begin in January, to honor Janus, the god of new beginnings. It was traditional to create an intention for something you would do as an offering to Janus, in the hopes of earning his favor for the rest of the year.

Fast forward to today when resolutions mostly seem to be another way we tell ourselves—or let society tell us—we're not good enough. About half of people who make resolutions even believe that they'll stick to them, and less than 10% actually do follow through. And then they feel like failures.

As Mark Twain said, *"New Year's Day... now is the accepted time to make your regular annual good resolutions. Next week you can begin paving hell with them as usual."*

What if instead of making—and likely forgetting—some grand New Year's resolutions, we just woke up each day, grateful that we woke up, and made a daily resolution to love ourselves and others just as we are?

Here's some resolutions I wish I would see:

Today I am going to love myself more.

Today I'm going to list at least three things I'm grateful for in my life.

Today I'm going to stop judging people based on their looks or their race or their sexual orientation or the fact that they don't have a home.

Today I'm going to do something I was saving for after I lost weight.

Today I'm going to put my iPad down, turn on some Abba and dance with my kids.

Today I'm going to avoid chemical shakes and cleanses and diets and instead I'm going to eat to nourish my body.

Today I'm going to go to yoga/dance class/swim/ride my bike and appreciate the strength and beauty of my body.

Today I'm going to sit still for 15 minutes and listen to my breath.

Today I'm going to recognize the perfection in myself and others.

You are perfect just the way you are, right now, today. I am perfect just the way I am. And even if we don't change one single thing about ourselves this year, we will still be perfect. And if that sounds crazy to you, make a New Year's resolution that you will say this to yourself over and over again until you believe it.

Happy New Year beautiful souls, embrace your perfection.

"We spend January 1 walking through our lives, room by room, drawing up a list of work to be done, cracks to be patched. Maybe this year, to balance the list, we ought to walk through the rooms of our lives...not looking for flaws, but for potential."

— Ellen Goodman

Reflection Questions:

- *What resolutions have you made over the years? How often did you succeed? Why or why not?*
- *If you accept yourself as perfect just the way you are, how does that change the way you move in the world? If you can't accept yourself as wholly perfect, in what areas do you find perfection?*

3 Things to Try Right Now if You Feel Anxious

145

You'll be surprised how well these work.

Anxiety is part of the human condition. There's not a person alive who hasn't experienced it. Anxiety includes feelings of nervousness, fear, and dread. Physical symptoms include lightheadedness, trembling, sweating, racing pulse, and difficult breathing.

Anxiety is generally episodic. You might become anxious before a speech or a test or get triggered by something specific. This form of stress can lead to a full-blown panic attack; that's why it's important to try to manage your anxiety as soon as it starts.

Here are three easy to remember techniques you can try next time you feel anxious. They can be easily done, whether you're at home, at work, on a plane, or anywhere anxiety strikes.

Square Breathing

If it's hard to catch your breath or your heart is racing, square breathing can help you lower your heart rate and return to your normal breathing patterns.

Sit up straight and lengthen your spine, lining your neck up with your spine.

Close your eyes.

Blow all the air out of your lungs in a big exhale, as if you are blowing out birthday candles.

Inhale slowly for the count of four.

Hold your breath for the count of four.

Exhale slowly for the count of four.

Hold your breath again for the count of four.

Repeat until you feel calmer. If you lose your place, re-straighten your spine, and start over.

The 5–4–3–2–1 Technique

Use this technique to ground yourself and focus your racing mind on something concrete.

Take one to three slow, deep breaths.

Look around and identify five things you see — examples: a chair or the light fixture. Keep your attention on each item for a couple of breaths.

Identify four things you can touch and use your fingers to create a tactile connection with the objects for a couple of breaths — examples: your hair or your shoe.

Identify three things you hear and focus on the sounds for a few seconds — examples: the furnace or traffic.

Identify two things you can smell — examples: your shampoo or a flower.

Identify one thing you taste. Example: coffee or toothpaste.

End with five slow, deep breaths.

Progressive Relaxation

This tactic can be particularly effective if you feel like your muscles are tense.

Starting with your feet, inhale and clench the muscles in your feet and toes tightly and hold for a few seconds.

Exhale and slowly relax those muscles.

Repeat the exercise, moving up through the calves, thighs, hips/glutes, back, stomach, chest, shoulders, arms, hands/fingers, neck, and face.

End by inhaling and simultaneously clenching all the muscles in the body, hold for 5–10 seconds, then exhale and relax.

Reflection Questions:

- *What makes you feel anxious? Is it generalized, or tied to specific events? Where do you feel anxiety in your body?*
- *Think of the last time you felt super anxious. How did you finally start to feel better?*

Did you like this book? Show the love and leave me a review. Reviews are like puppies, they make you feel happy.

About the Author

Rose Bak has been obsessed with books since she got her first library card at age five. She is a passionate reader with an e-reader bursting with thousands of beloved books.

Rose lives in the Pacific Northwest with her family, and special needs dogs. In addition to writing, she also teaches accessible yoga and loves music. Sadly, she has absolutely no musical talent, so she mostly sings in the shower.

A frequent contributor on Medium and other online magazine sites, Rose covers topics such as personal growth, aging, mental health, mindfulness, yoga, personal finance, and humor.

Although Rose enjoys writing both fiction and nonfiction, romance novels have always been her favorite guilty pleasure, both as a reader and an author. Rose's contemporary romance books focus on strong female characters over age 35 and the alpha males who love them. Expect a lot of steam, a little bit of snark, and a guaranteed happily ever after.

Be sure to join Rose's mailing list. Click here[1] to be the first to hear about all the latest releases and sales. Or follow Rose on social media @AuthorRoseBak.

---

1. https://bit.ly/rosebaknews

Other Books by Rose Bak

The Diamond Bay Series

Brand New Penny

Fresh as a Daisy

Right as Rain

The Good with Numbers Holiday Novella Series

Love Unmasked

The Thanksgiving Scrooge

Maid for Christmas

Countdown to Love

Valentine's Lottery

The Oliver Boys Band Series

Until You Came Along

Rock Star Teacher

Rock Star Writer

Rock Star Neighbor

Beach Wedding

Together Again

** Be sure to join Rose's mailing list. Click here[1] to be the first to hear about all the latest releases and sales. **

---

1. https://bit.ly/rosebaknews